ON THE IVORY STAGES

ON THE IVORY STAGES

THEODORE DALRYMPLE

MIRABEAU PRESS

Published by Mirabeau Press

PO Box 4281

West Palm Beach, FL 33401

ISBN: 978-1-7357055-8-3

First Edition

MIRABEAU

I labour by singing light
Not for ambition or bread
Or the strut and trade of charms
On the ivory stages
But for the common wages
Of their most secret heart.
Not for the proud man apart
From the raging moon I write
On these spindrift pages…

In My Craft or Sullen Art, Dylan Thomas

PREFACE TO AN INTRODUCTION

I have no procrustean theory to propound, no simple principle
or principles by means of which all human life may be made
clear or understood. Would life not be boring if such principles
could be found, and everything therefore decided in advance
of further thought or investigation?

It wasn't until I was in my mid-sixties that I liked a bargain. Then, as is the case with many people as they approach old age, I was seized by the prospect, or at least the possibility, of poverty. I saw myself crippled with arthritis, huddled round a miserable fire in a vain attempt to keep warm, something that not even a tropical sun would achieve, so thin would be my blood. All expenditure, at least on anything that had no resale value, would be spendthrift and had to be reduced to a minimum (with the partial exception to this dismal attitude the purchase of food and drink). Recently, I had the great and deeply satisfying triumph of having bought two packets of wholemeal pitta bread in my local supermarket for 7 pence each, marked down because their expiry date had been reached. They lasted me two weeks and were by no means disagreeable to eat when toasted with cheese.

Thus it was that I came to buy Gavin Maxwell's book *The Rocks Remain* for a mere 99 pence in a charity shop. The book, published in 1963, must once have been cherished, for it had been carefully covered in a mylar coat to prevent damage to its cover. I presume it had been inherited by someone who did not want it and who killed two birds with one stone by disembarrassing himself of it *and* donating to charity.

But did *I* really want it? — that was the question. After all, I am not exactly short of unread books in my house. However, circumstances conspired to encourage me to buy it. I had stepped out of my house, unusually with no book in my hand, and I had an appointment for which I might be kept waiting: precisely the reason why I seldom leave home without a book. My need for one had become urgent.

Even in my crabbed old age 99 pence did not seem to me

excessive. I suspected, even, that the book would cost several hundred per cent more to buy elsewhere: though buying and selling are quite different matters, of course, besides which I have never sold a book in my life and would rather sell my socks. But if I did not want the book and would not sell it, what advantage to me was its cheapness?

Nevertheless, I bought it, having long ago learned a lesson contradictory to my present attitude toward purchase, namely that one regrets what one didn't buy far more than what one did. Besides, I had read the first few pages in the shop and sensed at once that I would be able to suck some sustenance from the book, like a bee visiting a flower.

On page three, for example, Maxwell describes how he 'was engaged upon lengthy but not always leisurely research on certain aspects of twentieth-century Moroccan history.' This came as something of a surprise to me, as the author was best-known (at least to me) for his book about his life with otters, *Ring of Bright Water*, after the completion of which, not yet famous and not yet having sold more than a million copies, he went to stay in Marrakech: rather a change from a remote island in the west of Scotland. He rented a shabby room in the medina of Marrakech, where he tried to write:

> The single electric light-bulb dangling from the high ceiling gave a light inadequate for writing, and I bent low over the table. 'Hadj Abdullah ou Bitu, grand caid of the Haha,' I wrote carefully, 'was sent for to the Sultan's palace, where he was given the choice of a cup of poisoned tea or starvation to death while publicly exhibited in an iron… '

This rather unpleasant choice — I discussed by telephone the pros and cons of each with a friend — seemed to me an almost perfect metaphor for the choice the British government confronted in the condition of the British economy. The choice is always between immediate pain or pain in the future, and electoral politics being what they are, the latter always prevails, though pain supposedly in the future is often almost immediate. At any rate, the choice put me rather in mind of Robert Frost's famous lines:

> Some say the world will end in fire,
> Some say in ice…

While Maxwell was in Marrakech, he felt a strong earth tremor: a pale reflection of an earthquake in Agadir, a hundred and fifty miles away, that virtually destroyed that city and killed 10,000 of its 50,000 inhabitants. Maxwell accompanied the king, Mohammed V, to the stricken city, along with a party of diplomats and journalists. His description of the devastation was memorably graphic, but perhaps what struck me most, being so preoccupied with our present psychological and cultural conjunction (as most of us always are) was a clause that he put in parenthesis as he described a refugee camp the party visited:

> The orderly rows of tents, the green turf, the strolling ambassadors (some of whom were taking photographs of each other against suitable backgrounds), the royal presence and the extravagant greeting accorded to him, all combine to impart to this camp an air almost of fête.

The ambassadors taking photographs of each other, presumably on each other's behalf, against a background of human catastrophe, implied that it was really *their* presence that was most important to them in this scene. And I thought, perhaps this gives the glimpse of an answer to a question that I had long been asking myself: does technology call forth inclination or does inclination call forth the use to which technology is put? Did all the bile and venom that one sees expressed on the internet and the social media[1] exist before their advent, waiting only to emerge like a beast from its lair? Or did the mere possibility and ease of expressing it call it into being?

The selfie is no doubt the icon of our age: me and the Taj Mahal, me and St Basil's Cathedral, etc., the foreground being so much more important than the background. Well, this narcissism seems to have been current in 1960, at least, though more difficult, for technological reasons, to satisfy. Remember, moreover, that the ambassadors were probably highly educated and of high social class in their respective countries, so that their narcissism was not that of people wounded by their own unimportance.

But of course, a single clause in parenthesis is of limited evidential value in deciding what is probably an undecidable question. I still don't know the answer to it.

Certainly, the most succinct comment that I ever saw on what might be called *selfie culture* was in a (to me) unexpected place: a cartoon in the Bahreini English-language newspaper. It showed an open coffin in a church before the funeral. One

---

[1] Actually, the anti-social media.

of the mourners, with a smile on his face, was taking a selfie with the corpse.

This in turn reminded me of one of the most terrible photographs I have ever seen. It was in a French biography of the late dictator of Libya, Colonel Gaddafi. A young man, dressed in smart and freshly-laundered white clothes, was posing with an expression of pure happiness beside Gaddafi's corpse, already beginning to bloat from decomposition. The young man looked as if it was the proudest day of his life.

I don't suppose that I have to say that I had not the slightest political sympathy with or for Colonel Gaddafi: he was a man of pure malevolence. But his death was appalling: cruel, savage, brutal. No one should die as he died. To rejoice in the presence of someone done to death in this fashion would be dehumanising if it were not so very human.

We are the only species that can be appalled by itself.

If I were to be asked to name the greatest play of the twentieth century that is known to me (unlikely as it is that anyone would ask me such a fatuous question), I would reply, if given no time to think about it, *The Fire Raisers*, by Max Frisch. It was first performed in Zurich in 1958 and in London in 1961 and published in English exactly sixty years ago as I write this.

The title of the play in German was *Biedermann und die Brandstifter*, that is 'Biedermann and the Arsonists'. Biedermann is the central character, central because he is emblematic of a whole way of life and petty-mindedness. His very name suggests in German a certain narrowness of moral outlook, the kind that thinks that morality consists wholly of compliance with legal obligations and other formalities. Within these bounds he is upright; but if not evil himself, he has no place from which to resist evil and therefore allows evil to triumph.

Biedermann is a bourgeois, the head of a firm that makes and sells a lotion with false claims to make hair grow back again. Biedermann is perfectly aware that the claims are false: 'The good people who rub our hair tonic on their bald patches,' he says, 'might as well use their own urine.'

Here, succinctly, are the false promises of our consumer society, in which the unnecessary is sold to the insolvent. Unfortunately, the likely alternative to this society is worse.

Biedermann's cynicism, which he hardly recognises as such, is not all that can be said against him. He ruthlessly sacks the co-inventor (if that is quite the word for it) of his product, a man called Knechtling, meaning little servant, the moment that he has no further use for him; and he will not listen to the appeals of his wife, who has three children to feed. He simply tells her to go to her lawyer if she contests the dismissal. Humanity and justice mean nothing to him, only procedure is important. One cannot say that this frame of mind has disappeared entirely from the world.

The town in which Biedermann lives has recently been plagued by an outbreak of arson. There are fires everywhere, presumed to have been started by itinerant hawkers. One such itinerant arrives at Biedermann's house, and at first Biedermann refuses point blank to see him, but the itinerant, Schmitz, manages to insinuate himself into Biedermann's presence. He is a very large man, formerly a heavyweight wrestler, and tattooed (when Frisch wrote his play, this would have been enough to warn anyone that he was far from respectable, probably with a criminal past, a signal that, alas, has lost its meaning).

Schmitz spins a yarn — perhaps it is true — about his impoverished childhood, and by a mixture of intimidation and appeals to Biedermann's shallow sentimentality, he makes himself part of the household. Biedermann's wife, the subservient hausfrau, Babette, is a little more clear-sighted about Schmitz than her husband but quite unable to influence his conduct, though he himself is very weak when he is not bullying. Biedermann ends not only by offering Schmitz food, but by putting him up in the attic.

It becomes more and more obvious that Schmitz is one of the fire-raisers. He resists, very easily, Biedermann's feeble attempts to expel him from the house, the latter mistaking his own cowardice for generosity and good manners, another of his external guides to morality. Schmitz introduces an accomplice, Eisenring, into the house, and he also takes up residence in the attic. The pair of them bring drums of petrol into the house, and with a pusillanimous pretence first not to believe that it is petrol, and then to find it amusing, Biedermann refuses to see what is plain before his eyes. Indeed, he helps Eisenring to prepare the fuses with which his own house is obviously going to be set alight. And finally, on the very night the house is to be burnt down, Biedermann invites the two arsonists to a grand dinner of roast goose with chestnut stuffing and fine wine, to try and deflect their plans by a show of friendship.

Biedermann has ordered that there be no silver, no finger bowls, no damask table linen, no candelabras, at the dinner, because he does not want to embarrass his lower class 'guests', but they soon ask for the accoutrements of a bourgeois dinner party, and he orders that they should be brought.

The final scene takes place in Hell, where Schmitz and Eisenring are revealed to have been the Devil and Beelzebub. In Hell, Biedermann and Babette express the wish that everything should return to what it was before, only richer and better, that is to say with 'tall, modern buildings, gleaming with glass and chrome' — rather like Frankfurt, in fact. Biedermann says, 'To be quite frank, I must say it's a blessing it was burnt down, a positive blessing, from a town-planning point of view...'

It is not possible in a short summary to do justice to the brilliant suggestiveness and profundity of this most entertaining, though alarming, play. Perhaps the most important speech of the play is that of Eisenring when he says:

> Joking is the third best method of hoodwinking people. The second best is sentimentality. The kind of stuff our Schmitz goes in for — a childhood with charcoal burners, the forest, an orphanage, the circus [in which he performed and which was burned down], and so forth. But the best and safest method — in my opinion — is to tell the plain and unvarnished truth. Oddly enough. No one believes it.

This last is an obvious reference to *Mein Kampf*, in which Hitler did not conceal what he purposed to do — but no one took it seriously, so mad and evil was it.

The whole play is an allegory of the slide into

totalitarianism facilitated by people who believed that goodness is a purely formal quality, who are concerned only for themselves and who are too cowardly to see the obvious, let alone oppose or resist it. Through pusillanimity, indeed, they come to embrace what will destroy them, their future destroyers employing intimidation and appeals to sentimentality to gain their dominance, while at the same time taking over dinner tables set with silver, finger bowls, damask table linen and candelabras.

The brilliance of the play, however, is that, while it refers to a particular historical situation, that of the coming of communism, it also lays bare a universal problem, that of the slippery slope. At what point do we oppose what is wrong?

In every institution nowadays — hospitals, schools, large businesses, government departments, worst of all universities — administrative Schmitzes and Eisenrings pullulate and insinuate themselves into positions of power, also by a mixture of intimidation and appeals to sentimentality. At what point does one revolt and try to eject them? At what point is it too late? Politeness requires that, *à la* Biedermann, we never call them names such as mediocrities, megalomaniacs, careerists and so forth, and therefore they are enabled to spread their evil, their poison. We are all Biedermanns now and in the end (insofar as anything in history can be called an end), the whole town, country and civilisation will burn down.

If there are modern allegories more brilliant, of wider application, than that of Frisch (who, incidentally, was not himself particularly foresighted about Nazism, which biographical fact gives to the play an element of *mea culpa*), I do not know it.

11

Karl Marx's *The Eighteenth Brumaire of Louis Napoleon* is often described as a work of brilliant social and political analysis, polemic at its most accurate and excoriating. To me, however, Marx is like a clever know-it-all bore, as I was in my youth (at least, I thought myself clever). There is a certainty to his judgment that would be tolerable in a short article in a newspaper of known bias but is intolerable in an extended essay of more than a hundred pages. Marx is not so much a dialectician as a monological preacher calling down anathema on everyone but himself.

Throughout the essay, Marx assumes that people think what it is in their material interest to think, no doubt an observation of some sociological or psychological validity, but Marx elevates it into an epistemological principle, in which case the question arises in logic as to what material interest his own thought corresponds. In a certain sense, he is like Freud: everyone other than Freud needs an analyst, since uniquely Freud is able to analyse himself, just as Marx, uniquely, is able to think without material interest to guide him. Marx sees parasitism everywhere except in his own relationship to the factory-owning Engels.

For Marx, perhaps not surprisingly in view of the proportion of his life spent in libraries, abstractions are more real than people. He evinces no interest in actual people, except as bearers of social and economic class. He mentions innumerable persons in his polemic, but with the possible exception of Louis Napoleon, upon whom he heaps his vituperation, he does not pause to describe anyone's character, for such he would regard as irrelevant because for him people are marionettes controlled by social or economic forces acting as puppet-master. He is a great stereotyper and hypostasiser: social class has for him more reality than a mere human being. The bourgeoisie does this, the bourgeoisie does that, or it fails to do what it ought to do if it were to fulfil its historical role. *The people* were, almost by definition, opposed to the bourgeoisie, which mysteriously retained control of society despite being utterly stupid or blind to its own interests:

> ... the French bourgeois, whose skill, knowledge, mental insight and intellectual resources reach no farther than the end of his nose...

The continued rule of the bourgeoisie is all the more mysterious because of:

> ... the simple egoism which always inclines the ordinary bourgeois citizen to sacrifice the general interest of his class to this or that private motive.

Since by definition the ordinary bourgeois must be the most numerous bourgeois, the rule of the bourgeoisie must be maintained by the extraordinary bourgeois either in the interest of themselves as individuals or their class as a whole. If the latter, they are philanthropic as well as far-seeing, but if the former the bourgeoisie is either not a class or membership of a class does not determine thought and action.

Ultimately, Marx is superstitious if not outright religious. 'The task of the French Revolution,' he writes, 'was to destroy all separate, local, territorial, urban and provincial powers in order to create the civil unity of the nation.' But is a revolution the kind of entity that can have a task, and if so who or what is the taskmaster? Clearly, it is not the will of Man, or men, that sets the task. Who or what, then? How are the tablets brought down from Sinai that decree the course of human affairs? Marx is a monotheist atheist, or atheist monotheist, the God being History.

He is also not a very nice man, resentment and bloodthirstiness bubbling not very far below the surface — the surface being one of insult, disdain, contempt, and so forth, praise being offered in strictly homeopathic doses to those in some way in agreement with or useful to Marx's argument. And here is a passage from this work that goes some way to explaining why his followers were so bloodthirsty once in power (though perhaps the causation runs in the other direction, that it was his bloodthirstiness that attracted his followers in the first place):

> In the first French revolution the rule of the Constitutionalists was followed by the rule of the Girondins, and the rule of the Girondins by the rule of the Jacobins. Each of these parties leaned on the more progressive party. As soon as it had brought the revolution to the point where it was unable to follow it any further, let alone advance ahead of it, it was thrust aside by the bolder ally standing behind it and sent to the guillotine. In this way, the revolution moved in an ascending path.

There we have it! Progress by guillotine! The more we guillotine, the greater the progress! Note also that Marx, who claimed that his theory did not make use of sentimental ideas of morality but was a purely scientific theory of historical inevitability, uses words such as *progressive* and *higher* that make sense only in a scale of moral evaluation. Marx may have been brilliant, but he was not too bright when it came to logical consistency. Since few of us are fully consistent, perhaps this is not a devastating criticism, but even when we make allowances, the passage that I have quoted is surely enough to make our blood run cold, especially in the light of what was subsequently done in the name of Marxism.

My copy of this work, incidentally, is second-hand and somewhat worn, with quite a few passages underlined by the attentive previous owner, including such gems, which presumably the previous owner wanted to commit to memory, as 'A joint programme was drafted, joint election committees set up, and joint candidates put forward'. The guillotine passage I have just quoted, however, was *not* underlined by him, presumably as being unworthy of special notice by comparison with the drafting of a joint programme. Here we see the soul of the apparatchik in the making.

The most famous passage in *The Eighteenth Brumaire* comes near the beginning:

> Men make their own history, but not of their own free will; not under circumstances that they themselves have chosen but under the given and inherited circumstances with which they are directly confronted.

This, in part, is portentous cliché. Could one imagine a life into which people were born in circumstances freely chosen by them before they were born? However, it does not follow from the fact that they were born into particular circumstances that they are not free. I was born into an English-speaking country, and the language that I use and in which I think is therefore English. I inherited the grammatical rules that I did not make myself and which I must follow if I want to make myself understood: likewise the vocabulary. I did not choose that table should mean table. But it does not follow from this that what I say is completely predetermined. In this case, obedience to necessity really is the precondition of freedom, to adapt slightly one of Engels' dicta. Without rules, there could be no freedom of expression because there would be nothing to express. So Marx manages to be both portentous and wrong.

He continues, 'The tradition of the dead generations weighs like a nightmare on the minds of the living.' In this, Marx is very modern. In such historiography there is only injustice, misery and exploitation, no achievement or happiness. One wonders why humanity bothered to reproduce itself, and if the answer given is that it was prey to irresistible sexual urges, one might then wonder why it did not strangle all newborn babes in the cradle, so grim was their future. Who would condemn anyone to live in a perpetual nightmare?

One passage, however, would gladden the heart of any conservative who believed in limited government (though not the kind of anarchy that Marx proposed as the denouement of all history, the withering away altogether of the state):

Taxation is the source of life for the bureaucracy... for the whole executive apparatus... On all sides, therefore, it calls forth the direct interference of the state power... Finally, it produces an unemployed surplus population... which accordingly grasps at state office as providing a kind of respectable charity, thus provoking the creation of state posts.

One might say all this of the incontinent expansion of tertiary education of late decades.

Many people (of whom I am one) find a charm in books that bear the signature of their author. I am at a slight loss to make this charm appear rational. An author's signature does not make a bad book good or add any lustre to its contents. In a world of perfect rationality, we should value a book strictly according to its contents, or perhaps according to its beauty as an artifact. Instead, we often value highly even an ugly, mass-produced book of no literary distinction purely because it contains a dedication by its author. Why? I am no believer in ghostly emanations that cling to physical objects. Perhaps with supersensitive modern technology, it might be possible to find traces of an author's DNA on a book that he must have handled to sign it, but what would this avail us? Yet something of the mystique of a signed or dedicated copy remains to the susceptible, no doubt a hangover from romanticism. Probably the feelings induced by the association of objects with the persons who have handled them — Napoleon's toothpicks or Dickens' quill, for example — are inexpungeable.

I had not heard of Robert Lynd until one day (in Shrewsbury) I came across for sale one of his books, *Searchlights and Nightingales*, published in 1939, with the dedication, 'To Harold Warren from Robert Lynd, 30/11/39'.[2] But I soon discovered that Robert Lynd had been a distinguished essayist, a selection of whose work had received the accolade of publication in the *Everyman* series, an implicit claim to his status as at least a minor classic.

Robert Lynd was born in 1879 to a Presbyterian minister in Northern Ireland, in a household in which whistling and picking fruit (presumably for the pleasure of eating it) were regarded as sinful. He died five days before I was born.

Like many a person who rejects a narrow upbringing, he adopted an equal but opposite faith, becoming an ardent Irish nationalist, a member of Sinn Fein, a republican and socialist, though never himself an advocate of violence. For thirty-two years he wrote a weekly essay for the *New Statesman* under the name of *Y.Y.*, that is to say Ys or Wise. Notwithstanding his Irish nationalism, he lived all his adult life in London or thereabouts and had an elegant home in Hampstead, in which was held James Joyce's wedding reception.

Lynd's essays are very un-strident in tone, unexpectedly so in a man of such definite political opinions: they are, rather, those of an amused, sceptical observer of the follies of mankind, as well as a recorder of the small pleasures of

---

[2] The only Harold Warren of the time whom I have been able to trace was a man who graduated from the Royal Academy of Dramatic Art in 1932. Whether he had a subsequent career, or even whether he was the Harold Warren of the dedication, I do not know.

existence. Though a socialist, his pleasures are clearly not of the proletarian kind, but rather of the upper middle-class of his time. His tastes are fastidious (and expensive), and his prose style elegant. His socialism is of the kind that regrets that the finer things of life are not available to everyone, rather than of the more modern kind that denies that the finer things of life really are finer, nor does he allow the thought that their fineness owes at least something to their very exclusivity. Champagne would not be champagne if everyone drank it all the time.

In his day, Robert Lynd was famous, at least in educated circles, and not only in England. He could be very amusing: his essay *On the Average Man* in this book made me laugh. First, Lynd mocks the very idea of the average man to which, however, we are all inclined to resort from time to time. 'He is,' Lynd writes, 'according to reports, 5 feet 7 3/4 inches high, and weighs 11 stone 1 pound. He has brown hair and eyes, and his size in shoes is 8. Of these shoes he has two pairs, and each pair costs ten shillings. His size in hats in 6 7/8 - 7, and he has one child. He is 33 years old, and, at the age of 27 years and 4 months, he married a woman who at the time was 25 years and 6 months old…'

As Lynd points out, as soon as he reaches the age of 34, he ceases to be the average man — averageness is then as fleeting a quality as modernity in a world of change. 'But,' asks Lynd, 'even if the average man did exist, would it be worth discovering him?'

> Few of us would call in an average man as a doctor or would care to be defended by an average man in the law-

courts… The average man, I will agree, is often well spoken of in a vague way. We say: 'The average man is a decent fellow,' or 'The average man is fundamentally sound,' or 'The average man is kind to animals.'

'But,' continues Lynd, 'if the average man existed, he would soon discover that, while everyone speaks well of him, no one has any use for him.'

Lynd's principal genre, the short literary essay of about six to eight pages, collected in many volumes, is not now fashionable and he has fallen out of favour, as most authors must. The nearest modern equivalent known to me is Simon Leys, the brilliant Belgian-Australian sinologist who, in addition to his razor-sharp analyses of the Chinese Cultural Revolution, was a wonderful and witty literary essayist. But the appetite for the genre is now limited.

Lynd is light and I suppose one must add middle-brow, and as one might expect in an oeuvre so extensive, his writing varies in quality (only a very mediocre writer is always at his best, Somerset Maugham says somewhere). But he is not always light or trivial. The book that I bought in Shrewsbury because of its dedication was signed less than three months into the cataclysmal Second World War and the essays in it were clearly written in the long shadow of the forthcoming war. The sixth essay in the book is titled *In Defence of the Trivial*. It starts:

A charming woman told me the other day that she has ceased going to parties. 'One doesn't feel in the mood for enjoying oneself, does one,' she said, 'with all these horrors going on everywhere. I went to the opera the other night, but the flavour seemed to have gone out of it, and I couldn't help feeling guilty when I thought of Spain and China and Austria. Don't you think going to operas and plays and cinema just now is rather like fiddling while Rome is burning?'

To this, Lynd has the perfect reply:

I asked her to name a century in which Rome was not burning — a century in which, if a man concentrated his thoughts on the miseries of mankind, he would not have been equally in doubt whether he had the right to enjoy himself.

There has always been enough oppression in the world to make sensitive people mourn, says Lynd. 'Yet, by some trick of double-mindedness, millions of the most kindly people have been able to get a good deal of enjoyment out of life.' It is moral exhibitionism to claim an inability to enjoy oneself on account of the miseries of the world, and while there is no new thing under the sun, such exhibitionism seems to be on the rise.

In another essay, *The Sky Is Blue*, Lynd reflects on how it is possible to enjoy oneself in the year 1939 under the shadow of war. (As this essay is near the beginning of the book, I suspect it was written early in that year.)

I turned on the wireless set and chose a station at random. Once more I was fortunate. Children were singing — singing as sweetly as any choir of birds, as any rain-fed stream wandering among grass and stones. How happy they sounded — with the natural happiness of childhood on which the future casts a shadow! It was a German song, and it was good to know that even German children live in a world on which the sun shines — a careless, innocent world, free from calamity. When the song was over, one gathered, however, that they were not ordinary German children but refugee children torn from their German homes. A girl in a sweet voice told in a charmingly foreign English what was being done for them...

My mother arrived in England from Germany almost to the month in which Lynd wrote this essay. I doubt that she ever sang, and by the time I knew her, she had absolutely no German accent whatever, a remarkable achievement for someone who didn't speak English until she was nineteen.

Despite having just read Robert Lynd's defence of taking pleasure in dark times, with which I strongly agreed, I was mildly irritated to read in Andrei Kurkov's *Diary of an Invasion* of the Ukrainian population's interest in the Eurovision Song Contest immediately before the Russian invasion of their country, which was clearly imminent.

Kurkov is probably the most famous writer living in Ukraine (I still have to halt myself from saying and writing *the* Ukraine, having been born and raised when the Soviet Union seemed immutable). He is Russian and writes in Russian, but he is a firm and unequivocal supporter of the Ukrainian cause.

His *Diary* starts in December, 2021, and continues until July, 2022, so there is no denouement (insofar as anything in history can be said to have denouement).

On 20 February, 2022, he wrote:

> Last week, Ukrainians were preoccupied not only with a possible Russian air-strike, but with the Eurovision song contest. In fact, there were more songs on T.V. than news items about a potential war. Ukrainians were choosing a candidate to represent Ukraine at the Eurovision in Italy.

Forgetting Lynd, and assuming that what Kurkov wrote was true, this irritated me.

Why? After all, present mirth hath present laughter, and what's to come is never sure. The majority of the Ukrainian population, indeed the Ukrainian government itself, had no influence on the Russians as to whether or not they would invade, so why not immerse themselves in entertainment? In a way, to do so is evidence of the power of resilience. But despite telling myself this, the irritation remained.

It was not distractions or entertainments in dark times that I objected to, but the nature of *this* distraction or entertainment, which I considered (without having seen it for myself) most likely to have been ersatz, garish, crude, vulgar, inartistic and in the worst possible taste. I imagined flashing lights, high-tech sets, shiny cheap-expensive costumes, the whole cynically industrialised nature of the whole contest, as well as the whipped-up hysteria accompanying it. I find such bad taste almost physically painful.

But who am I to decree what is good and bad taste? Why should millions of people not take pleasure where they can find it but where I can find none? What is true as against false or ersatz excitement, and what are the criteria for infallibly distinguishing between them? It would require hard thinking to develop such criteria, assuming that the distinction is one that could be made and which actually exists. I think I am just a snob.

Another passage in Kurkov's book arrested my attention. He describes how, having read *The Gulag Archipelago* while it was still forbidden to do so in the Soviet Union, he travelled round that still-existent country to talk to servants of the *ancien régime*. 'Listening to them, he says, 'I sometimes felt as if I had touched a hot stove with my unprotected finger.'

> One of the people who agreed to talk was Alexander Petrovich Smurov. I found him in the Crimea, near the town of Sudak where he lived in quiet retirement. In the now distant 1930s he had been one of the judges who had sentenced people without a court hearing. He spoke freely about how he had put his signature to death warrants for people about whom he knew practically nothing. To my question about the number of death sentences he had signed, he replied, "Perhaps three thousand, possibly more." This man was unafraid to recall to me what he had done. He was confident of his innocence. He spoke fondly of his youth and his enthusiasm for the Soviet cause.

This brought to mind the answer of the late historian, Eric

Hobsbawm, a convinced Marxist, who in answer to the question of whether he thought twenty million deaths in the Soviet Union were justified, replied that they would have been justified if the Soviet Union had turned out to be the paradise it was hoped to be. And he was a man who died, if not in the odour of sanctity exactly, at least in that of admiration.

Smurov's bland assurance of having done nothing wrong (again, I assume that Kurkov's depiction of him is accurate) is a chilling example of the flexibility of conscience under the influence of ideology, abstractions, a world outlook, which can overwhelm with ease what one would normally think of as human nature itself. Presumably Smurov did not carry out the killings himself and was to that degree protected from the tangible consequences of his own actions, but it is impossible that he did not know what the executions were like or how they were carried out. Was he merely saving his own skin by his zeal for death, or did he truly believe that what he was doing was right (or some combination of the two?). As Marx might have said, the relationship between the desire for self-preservation or advancement and belief in the cause was probably a *dialectical* one.

Where on the scale of human monsters does he lie? Is he worse than someone who ordered only two thousand such executions, but not as bad as someone who ordered four thousand? When one considers the monstrosity of a single unjust execution, say that of Mrs Edith Thompson, after a trial that was scrupulous by Soviet standards, one averts one's mind from the question.

Again, as with the attention given to the Eurovision Song Contest, one is confronted by the ability of the human mind to distract itself from reality, in the case of Smurov by the use of abstractions such as 'class enemies', abstractions that are themselves dependent on further abstractions such as *bourgeoisie* and *proletariat*. Of course, we need such abstractions, for thought would be impossible without them, but at least in the human sphere they are very dangerous when they prevail completely over apprehensions of the individuals whom we encounter in life.

My one and only visit to Pakistan was more than half a century ago. We had descended on the Khyber Pass, even then (before the political cataclysm unleashed in Afghanistan by the coup against good King Zahir Shah) dangerous to travel at night, gunfire starting at nightfall as promptly and reliably as cicadas stop chirping when the temperature goes down. We reached the fabled city of Peshawar, then only a tenth of its present size; we slept in a courtyard on charpoys, frame beds with jute netting, under the starry sky on a balmy night. It was so romantic that I could almost have written poetry.

A bit later, in the Murree Hills, we ordered a chicken curry in a tin-shack restaurant, our order followed immediately by the sound of someone clambering and clattering over the roof in pursuit of a fleeing chicken, the curry appearing an astonishingly short time after the squawking of the chicken ceased. The following morning, as we were walking in the Murree Hills, a young Pakistani man appeared in our path dressed in a dog-toothed sports jacket and cavalry twill trousers and addressed us in the most perfect upper-class English.

Pakistan, I surmise, has become a good deal more desperate since those far-off days, in large part because of the increase in its population. Karachi alone is now a city of 20 million, and the desperation (and resilience) of the place is recounted in a book by Samira Shackle, daughter of Pakistani immigrants to England, who returns regularly to Karachi to write from there. Her book is titled *Karachi Vice*.

A sentence in the first paragraph of the *Prologue* startled me. In 2012, Ms Shackle had just moved to Karachi for a time:

> I moved to Karachi in the aftermath of riots, arriving to smashed shop windows and the smell of burning tyres...[3] the city had been engulfed by protests against a YouTube video that made offensive statements against the Prophet Muhammad...The scale of the destruction was disproportionate to the offence itself.

What would have been the scale of the destruction *proportionate* to the offence itself? I rather doubt whether the author (who is now the editor of *The New Humanist*, the house journal of the Rationalist Association) is much in favour of riots defending the good name of the Prophet Muhammad.

Does looseness of language that disregards the corollary of what it says matter much? It would be difficult to prove one way or the other, at least if empirical effects were all that mattered, and not accuracy or precision for its own sake. I was reminded by the last sentence I have quoted above of the

---

[3] A sight, sound and smell with which I was familiar from Panama City, whither I had been sent from Haiti to report on the crisis there.

police spokesmen who say, in the aftermath of a murder or a robbery in which the victim was killed, that it was a senseless murder or a robbery that went tragically wrong: as if there were sensible murders or robberies that went nice and smoothly, I suppose the latter being when the robber gets away with the loot, leaving the robbed uninjured.

An English judge, sentencing a career criminal who had hit and killed a man whom he thought had had an argument with his girlfriend over a place in a queue, said 'It would have been bad enough if you had got the right person' — thus revealing that he, the judge, thought, at least implicitly, that there was a right person to 'get'. And if this is what judges think, the question is not why there are so many murders, but why there are so few?

The second chapter in the book (which consists of verbal sketches of the lives of residents of Karachi) is about Parveen, a teacher in an informal school, that both supplements and (for some) replaces the appallingly bad government schools. Parveen is a valiant person, living in a violent and impoverished part of the city (as most parts of it are), but eventually is forced by the gangster violence to move away. In this chapter, the children who attend her school are called *students*.

This, of course, is modern usage, and it has a hinterland of meaning. The word should really have been *pupil*, but this word has almost disappeared from the lexicon, with its implication of hierarchy. It implies also that a child *grows* into student-hood, gradually replacing directed by self-directed study. Of course, there is no precise date or time at which a pupil becomes a student, but to object on these grounds that there is no difference between the two is like arguing that there is no difference between a tall and a short man because there is no precise height at which a man becomes tall.

Behind the use of the word 'student' for a seven-year-old, say, is the idea that the pupil and the student are on a voyage of discovery together on a boat with no officers, that is to say no hierarchy. Naturally, a good teacher neither abuses his power nor needs to, but to pretend that he is not the child's superior in both knowledge itself and in knowing what the child ought to learn is to call into question the need for education in the first place. Why do children need to go to school at all if adults are not entitled, indeed obliged, to direct the path that children should follow, because they as adults know more?

However, I do not want to carp about this book, which is a very good one that successfully conveys to the reader the sheer pullulation of the city, with its vibrancy, misery and death. Reading it, one has the feeling that one would rather die than live there, at least unless one lived in the walled-off enclaves of the rich. However, the growth of the city suggests that this is a purely western reaction. The people of Karachi are not suicidal.

It is likely that many westerners think of Pakistanis as an undifferentiated mass, if not a mob, of fanatical Moslems, without much distinction between them, but this, of course, could hardly be more false: the hatreds and antagonisms between the ethnic and cultural groups who make up Pakistan's population are of murderous intensity. There is a chapter about two brothers who work to bring water, electricity and sanitation to a zone of the city, Orangi, that was first built chaotically to shelter the Urdu-speaking Mohajirs (the Moslem refugees from India during and after Partition, and also from East Pakistan during and after the war of Bangladeshi independence) but later also inhabited by Pushtun from the north-west attracted by the supposed opportunities of the city. This ethnic mixture is combustible, and each ethnic group has its political party. The Mohajirs' party, predominant in Orangi, is the Muttahida Qaumi Movement, a hybrid of social democracy and the Mafia. In such situations, not only geographic areas but occupations are divided ethnically, public transport, for example, being in the hands of the Pushtun. Bus drivers, all Pushtun, are in constant danger of assault and murder by the Mohajirs, or at least by the gunmen of the MQM, who claim to defend the interests of the Mohajirs. One of the brothers described in the chapter rode on the bus of a Pushtun driver who was murdered a few days later.

The division of occupations and areas in the Indian subcontinent by ethnic, cultural or religious groups has been imported into England by immigration. In the large town nearest me as I write this, all the taxi drivers are Punjabi Sikhs; in the large city thirty miles away, they are all Punjabi Moslems. Is this separation spontaneous, planned, informal or enforced? What would happen if a Sikh tried to be a taxi driver in the city or a Moslem in the town? I would like to know but am afraid to ask.

Of Orangi, the author says, 'The invisible lines separating people of different ethnicities become more obvious, sometimes physically demarcated on a map, where a single road might mark a sharp division.'

I thought of my small flat in Paris, not far from which is just such a road. On the one side are the eighteenth and nineteenth century buildings frequented by bourgeois bohemians: chichi bars and restaurants, art galleries, alternative health practitioners, etc.; on the other side, the hideous constructions in concrete of French fascisto-communist architects, inhabited by African immigrants in a colourful variety of costumes, with shops full of dried fish and plantains, exotic fruits and cheap spices. The wall between these two worlds is invisible but almost as effective as that between East and West Germany of old, a metaphysical wall, as it were, like something in a film by Buñuel.

I feel more at my ease among the Africans than among the young bobos.

Steven Runciman's three volume *A History of the Crusades* contains an implicit explanation of the attraction of books signed or dedicated by their authors, or once owned by famous or distinguished people. Runciman was a man who, without being a fully-fledged believer, was always interested in the occult and the paranormal, and he explains the development of the cult among early Christians of saintly relics:

> Authorities such as Prudentius and Ennolus taught that divine succour could be found at the grave [of the early Christian saints], and that their bodies should be able to work miracles. Men and women would now travel far to see holy relics. Still more, they would try to acquire one

to take it home and set it in their local sanctuary.

In the same way:

> To stand where those that we reverence once stood to see the very sites where they were born and toiled and died, gives us a feeling of mystical contact with them and is a practical expression of our homage.

Surely the desire for signed or dedicated copies of books, or those that once belonged to the famous (or infamous), partakes of an attenuated form of this mysticism?

As it happens, my copy of this three-volume work is what is called an *association copy*, that is to say it was once in the possession of, or associated with, a person of some note. In this case, it was a man called Ian Samuel, of whom I had not heard before I bought the books (in Tunbridge Wells). The internet permitted me to trace him with ease, the inscriptions of the books being as follows: Vol. 1, Ian Samuel, Cairo, 1951;[4] Vol. 2, Ian Samuel, Damascus; Vol. 3, Ian Samuel, Miswills House,[5] Turner's Hill, Surrey, Oct. 1954. I deduced from all this, correctly as it turned out, that Samuel had been a diplomat. I quote from the *Daily Telegraph* obituary:

---

[4] There is a rather charming sticker in the book also, from the Horus Bookshop, Cairo. It is interesting that an academic book published in 1951 should have been immediately available in Cairo.

[5] I was likewise able to trace Miswills House on the internet. It struck me as rather ugly, but its latest valuation was at £1.89 million. Its grounds are much more beautiful than the house.

Adrian Christopher Ian Samuel was born on August 20 1915 in Colchester and educated at Rugby and St John's College, Oxford, where he read modern languages. Deciding on a career in the Foreign Service, he learnt Arabic to add to his French, German, Spanish and Turkish; his first postings were to Beirut, Tunis and Trieste.

His career was interrupted by the war, and he became a bomber pilot. He sank a German submarine.

> … a U-boat was spotted three miles away. Despite heavy anti-aircraft fire from the surfaced submarine, he dived from 2,000 ft and dropped depth charges. His rear gunner saw the U-boat heel (sic) over and submerge. Then, as Samuel circled above, the submarine reappeared with the bows at an acute angle. He attacked again, and U-169, which had left Kiel to join a Seewolf group, sank vertically with all hands.

It is a tribute to the horrors of war that Samuel must have rejoiced at his success. Such is the effect of war on mentality, no doubt here with justification. Still, when one thinks of the men drowning in their steel tube…

> Soon afterwards… he was escorting an Atlantic convoy when he was forced to ditch. He managed to land [in water] close to a destroyer, and he and his crew were soon picked up.

It was after the war that he was posted first to Cairo and then Damascus, in the latter meeting the infamous spy and traitor Kim Philby, 'who lamented the loss of British operatives behind Soviet lines' — which he was instrumental in having brought about.

One's life in comparison has been tame. Dr Johnson once said that 'every man thinks meanly of himself for not having been a soldier, or not having been at sea,' and that is precisely what I thought of myself after having read Samuel's obituary.

One can surely deduce something of Samuel's character from the condition of the books. Despite having been transported from England to Cairo and Damascus, and back again, and also having almost certainly been read by Samuel with attention, they are, seventy years old, as new, almost as they came off the press. I might add that in those economically straitened years, the books were far better printed, on far better-quality paper, than they would have been today.

From the obituary, we learn that Samuel was a man who 'enjoyed good food, good wine and genial company.' While he must have kept his book fastidiously, he was no killjoy.

In 1987 he published an article in the *Spectator* (for which I was then occasionally writing myself). This article, important enough to be mentioned in his obituary, is of surprising relevance to today, thirty-five years later.

In 1984, aged 69, he suffered an episode of 'flu, after which he lost his sense of smell. He was told by neurologists that this was a rare complication of viral infections and that it was unlikely that his sense would ever return. This was particularly cruel for a man for whom good food and wine were a principal pleasure in life, and in the article, he related the unpleasantness of eating the various consistencies of tasteless cardboard. By the time he wrote the article, he had recovered his sense somewhat but far from completely. He could just about tell a gustatory hawk from a gustatory handsaw.

Oddly enough, until the Covid-19 epidemic, I had never really considered of the loss of the sense of smell (and what we usually call taste) very seriously. This was a failure of imagination on my part. I did not stop to think what it must be like having to eat without a sense of smell and solely to keep the bodily machine going in the same way as a locomotive fireman used to shovel coal into the engine.

When I thought about it, the reason for my mother-in-law's stubborn resistance to eating became clear. It could take an hour or more to take a few mouthfuls, and no matter what was put on the plate before her, including the things that she had loved, she complained that everything was *fade*, insipid. She was like a small child that would not eat its spinach.

Of course! She had lost her sense of smell because of her Alzheimer's disease, of which loss of that smell can be an early symptom. I understood now why she described eating as a *corvée*. I confess shamefacedly that I sometimes considered her stubbornness in not eating to be a mode of attracting attention, though I hope I never showed my irritation and impatience, despite the hours we spent coaxing her.

If only I had read and remembered in a journal for which I write the article by a remarkable man, whose copy of *A History of the Crusades* in three volumes I now possess.

The Book Bag, a short story by Somerset Maugham published

in 1932, begins:

> Some people read for instruction, which is praiseworthy, and some for pleasure, which is innocent, but not a few read from habit and I suppose that this is neither innocent nor praiseworthy. Of that lamentable company am I... My own thoughts, which we are told are the unfailing resource of a sensible man, have a tendency to run dry. Then I fly to my book as the opium-smoker to his pipe.

He goes on to say that he would rather read a train timetable than nothing at all.

In 1936, in an essay titled *Readers and Writers*, published in book form in *The Olive Tree*, Aldous Huxley writes:

> To a considerable extent, reading has become for almost all of us an addiction, like cigarette-smoking. We read, most of the time, not because we wish to instruct ourselves, but because reading is one of our bad habits... Deprived of their newspaper or a novel, reading-addicts will fall back on... those instructions for keeping the contents crisp which are printed on boxes of breakfast cereal.

Indeed so. But I am not accusing Huxley of plagiarism: condemnation of the vice or reading — of *over*-reading as one might call it — are to be found in Schopenhauer, who thought that books could prevent thought at least as much, or more than, they provoke or encourage it, thought being so painful to so many people. Still, the coincidence between Maugham and Huxley is interesting, as coincidences always are.

My copy of *The Olive Tree* bears the name S. Lushington on the half title page, written in a hand that I should adjudge not fully mature, and signed at Tenterden in December 1936. On the front pastedown is a fine engraved bookplate, printed with an elegance that one rarely sees these days. At what date this bookplate was designed and printed I do not know, but if it was in 1936, when S. Lushington, as I discovered, was 19, he was a very privileged youth, and moreover one with good taste.

Little research was required to discover that S. Lushinton was Stephen Lushington, born in Tenterden in 1917 to Lt. Col. Franklin Lushington, soldier and novelist. After Eton and Oxford, Stephen returned to Eton to teach. The war interrupted his career, to which he returned afterwards to teach at Westminster School for the rest of his active life. He died, as I learned in an obituary in *The Times*, in 2012 aged 95 — the same age at death as Ian Samuel.

Schoolmastering seems to me a noble profession, for a teacher must be aware that some of his pupils at least will outstrip him and become more famous or learned than he: indeed, it is one of his duties to try to prepare them to be so. It is therefore a life of selfless dedication to the advancement of civilization, as few professions are. But perhaps the selflessness is not entirely without regret. A brief interview can be found with Lushington on the internet, taken shortly before his death. He is slow to reply and clearly short of breath. The interviewer asks him whether he was pleased that some of his pupils went on to fame, and he said that he found it interesting but could not say that he was unselfish enough to have rejoiced at it. Was this the plain truth, or was it reluctance, even in the face of death, which he must have known was fast approaching, to praise himself? Was it a slightly melancholy avowal at the end of life of the relatively humble role of the schoolmaster?

Huxley was a wonderful essayist: amusing, erudite and opinionated (who wants to read an essayist who is always fair and judicious?). His essay on his grandfather known as Darwin's bulldog, *T.H. Huxley as a Literary Man*, made me laugh:

> Mr G.K. Chesterton has a genius for saying new and surprising things about old subjects. We are grateful to him for his originality. But there is such a thing as being too original by half… For example, in his stimulating little book, *The Victorian Age in Literature*, he says of Lord Macaulay and T.H. Huxley that 'they were more under the influence of their own admirable rhetoric than they knew. Huxley, especially, was much more a literary than a scientific man.'

Then Huxley says with his own admirable rhetoric:

> Being myself of the literary profession, I think I can guess how a fellow man of letters would arrive at the conclusion so boldly enunciated in Mr. Chesterton's book. The process is simplicity itself. All that is required is a little systematic and selective ignorance. Ostrich-like, one shuts one's eyes to the scientific achievements of one's

subject. One refrains from reading any of his technical papers... and one concentrates exclusively on his more accessible, his more specific literary productions. The result is that one comes, logically and inevitably, to the conclusion that 'Huxley, especially, was much more a literary than a scientific man.' Q.E.D. It is as evident as a proposition of Euclid.

Using such a method, says Huxley (and I am far from innocent of having used it myself), one could easily conclude that Einstein was much more a violinist than a mathematical physicist.

One of the essays in the book is about Benjamin Haydon, a figure who has always been attractive to me because he had, to quote the title of a recent biography of him, a genius for failure. I find failures more attractive than successes, perhaps because of a sense of fellow-feeling. Haydon and I are citizens of that populous country, the land of failures.

Poor Haydon! He was a man of parts, but his problem was that he wanted to be, and believed, almost to the point of delusion, he was, a great painter; but he needed precisely those gifts he did not possess to become one. All his life he struggled to be what he could never be, as someone with a tin whistle might try to be Mozart. He was possessed of a very strong personality, and the work by which he achieved minor immortality, his diary, demonstrated that he had literary talents had he but employed them fully. He even had an acute critical faculty with regard to painting other than his own; of Benjamin West's classical picture, for example, he wrote, 'The Venuses looked as though they had never been naked before,' to which Huxley rightly added, 'There is nothing more to be said.' Haydon's succinctness and powers of description of social events amounted almost to genius. Alas, he thought his genius lay in another field of endeavour. His struggle against failure, both private and public, caused him to cut his throat at the age of sixty, a tragic denouement of a life that had, after all, been dedicated to the pursuit of an ideal. Its magnificence was in its failure.

Dickens wrote briefly of Haydon's death, a few lines of evident humanity and genuine sorrow, but also of honesty:

> All his life he had utterly mistaken his vocation. No amount of sympathy with him and sorrow for him in his manly pursuit of a wrong idea for so many years… ought to prevent one from saying that he most unquestioningly was a very bad painter.

Surely it is time for an exhibition of Haydon's work. After all, it is by seeing the bad that one comes to appreciate the good at its true worth. Alas, no one will ever mount such an exhibition, among other reasons because he went in for vast historical canvases which would cost a fortune to transport. Only a person with a heart of stone, or rather with no visual taste or sense of the absurd, could look at his *Curtius Leaping into the Gulf* without laughing: somewhat guiltily, no doubt, in view of his suicide four years after it was painted.

There was a boy at school who belonged, hereditarily, to the Plymouth Brethren — the Exclusive branch of that peculiar sect, I think. He was ill-favoured by Nature, in fact ugly, and was pasty-faced from hiding away from the world when not at school. He was inclined to sweatiness and had spots, but not those common in adolescents, but little red excoriations as if he had been attacked by mites. He was, however, very clever, excelling in mathematics. He would also have been a good cricketer if his religion and his parents had allowed him to play out of school hours, but they thought that cricket, being enjoyable to him, was a snare and a delusion, which I suppose that, in common with all sport, it is. At any rate, his intercourse with us was slight and minimal, though I don't think that he was inherently unfriendly. It was just that we were unrighteous or worse, of the party of the Devil. Whether in later life he escaped the narrow sectarianism of his parents, or had a brilliant career, I do not know. We pitied rather than persecuted him; I grew up in an atmosphere of the most complete religious toleration, which I suppose may have been an indication of the unimportance, for good or ill, of religion to us.

I thought no more of the Plymouth Brethren until I read Edmund Gosse's wonderful memoir of growing up with a father (the eminent naturalist, Philip Henry Gosse, Fellow of the Royal Society), who was a rigid member of the sect. How accurate *Father and Son* is, I do not know; Henry James said that Gosse has a genius for inaccuracy. But still the memoir, even if some of it is downright fictional rather than inaccurate as a natural consequence of the fallibility of memory, is a small masterpiece.

I was much struck by the anecdote in which the young Gosse asks his father whether he may visit a neighbour, much,

I surmise, as the boy at school may have asked his parents whether he could play cricket. Gosse *père* told the young Edmund to pray to God to ask Him whether he might go on the visit, fully expecting God to return him an answer forbidding it, for it was evident that Gosse *père* did not want him to go, disapproving of frivolous activities such as social visits. So Edmund prayed, but the answer came back that God said that young Edmund might visit the Browns. The father was hoist with his own petard: he could hardly tell his son that God had said no such thing without destroying his son's faith in the worth or authenticity of prayer.

More recently, I contracted (morally, not financially) to give a talk to the Bridgnorth Historical Society, my fourth to that august body, the three previous having been on the parliamentary election of 1852, full of fun, fights and bribery; on the early days of the *Bridgnorth Journal* (which, in its current incarnation, my neighbour calls the *Gerbil*), very distinguished, for example carrying the first printing of the texts of some of the lectures, still in print, that Lord Acton gave in the town; and on the life and work of the 'learned and eloquent' Richard Baxter, the seventeenth century divine and prolific author, who lived for a short time in the cottage four doors from my house. The subject of my fourth lecture was to be the Reverend George Bellett, long time rector (1835-1870) of St Leonard's church, opposite my house, and author of *The Antiquities of Bridgnorth*. The scion of an Irish Anglican family, Bellett's brother, John Gifford Bellett, was one of the founders of the Plymouth Brethren. In preparation for my talk, I read *A History of the Plymouth Brethren*, a copy of which I happened to possess, by a man rejoicing in the splendid name of W. Blair

Neatby. It was published in 1901 by the commercial publisher, Hodder and Stoughton, who presumably thought the book of sufficient interest to the general public to be profitable. In those days, religious controversies retained their salience for numbers of people.

It is not easy for persons such as I who are unversed in theology to follow or be captivated by the bitter disputes by which the Plymouth Brethren were soon riven. There never was a precise founding of the sect; rather, it emerged (largely from Irish Protestantism) from a growing feeling in the first quarter of the nineteenth century that there was no theological or scriptural justification for a caste of clergy completely separate from the laity: rather, every person was qualified and entitled to administer the sacraments. The movement, however, fell under the sway of a man called John Nelson Darby, also Anglo-Irish, who soon established his charismatic dictatorship over others, leading inevitably to fissions, anathemata and excommunications — an odd, but perhaps, predictable denouement of what started out as an anticlerical movement to unite all Christians. To adapt slightly Shigalyov's dictum in Dostoyevsky's novel, *The Possessed*, 'Starting from ecclesiological anarchy, the Plymouth Brethren arrived at absolute papism.'

Darby apparently had a very strong personality, and I think this is evident from the photographic frontispiece in Neatby's book, showing a man with the scowl of a prophet, in whose company one would not care to make jokes. He was severe, rigid and convinced, a man who squashed doubt, including his own, by means of dogma and inquisition. For a time, he prevailed over even so brilliant a man as Francis William

Newman, younger brother of the famous cardinal-to-be, who was mathematician, philosopher, philologist and proponent of vegetarianism. Newman went out with others (including George Bellett's brother) to Baghdad as a missionary but, unsurprisingly, converted no one; he subsequently published an English-Arabic dictionary and a verse translation of *The Iliad*. Clearly, anyone who could have exercised a hold over such a man, even if only temporarily, was remarkable. Newman later wrote:

> In spite of the strong revulsion I felt against some of the peculiarities of this remarkable man [Darby], I for the first time in my life found myself under the dominion of a superior... Henceforth, I began to ask: what will *he* say to this and that?... From seeing his action and influence, I have learnt, that if it is dangerous to a young man (as it assuredly is) to have *no* superior mind to which he may look up with confiding reverence, it may be even more dangerous to think that he has found such a mind: for he who is most logically consistent, though to a one-sided theory, and most ready to sacrifice self to that theory seems to ardent youth the most assuredly trustworthy guide.

Charisma is the enemy of thought and judgment, though we complain of some politicians' lack of it.

The bitterness of Darby's theological disputes was astonishing — there was real *odium theologicum* about them, filled as they were with rhetorical violence about arcane matters over which we should not now concern ourselves very deeply, but which for the Victorians were of immense significance. Darby disputed with his erstwhile friend and companion 'in the work', B.W. Newton, the question of whether any part of Christ's earthly sufferings was attributable to his nature as a man who therefore had Original Sin which he had to expiate by means of suffering. There was a pamphlet war between them, Darby insulting Newton and calling him satanic. Thereafter, they did not speak for fifty years, though they had been very close. Christian charity is more easily preached than practised.

Of course, this *odium theologicum* can exist without theology. Psychologically, at any rate, the disputes of Marxist sects over *true* Marxism were very similar.

No stronger, or stranger, instance of the effect of charisma on a rational man, or at least on a man who believed himself to be rational, could be found than that of D.H. Lawrence's effect upon Betrand Russell. The latter, after all, was no mental or moral weakling: he was prepared to go to prison for the sake of his opposition to the First World War.

Russell met Lawrence in 1915, at Lady Ottoline Morrell's country house. The seemingly desiccated logician there encountered the passionate irrationalist.

They both opposed the war, though for different reasons, as Russell later discovered. The effect that Lawrence had on Russell was immediate, but it cannot be said that Russell was always susceptible to charisma. When he met Lenin in 1920, for instance, he found him dull, dogmatic, schoolmasterly in the worst possible fashion, and with a very strong streak of cruelty.

Of his relations with Lawrence, Russell later wrote, in *Portraits from Memory* published in 1956:

> What at first attracted me to Lawrence was a certain dynamic quality and a habit of challenging assumptions that one is apt to take for granted. I was already accustomed to being accused of undue slavery to reason and I thought perhaps he could give me a vivifying dose of unreason.

One of Lawrence's letters brought Russell to the verge of despair:

> It isn't in the least true [wrote Lawrence] that you, your basic self, want ultimate peace. You are satisfying in a false way your lust to jab and strike.

Here, in essence, was the Nietzschean view that altruism is but disguised weakness and thirst for revenge, a view that is either so untrue as to be silly, or true only by definition, the lowest form of truth.

> Either satisfy [that lust to jab and strike] in a direct and honourable way, saying 'I hate you all, liars and swine, and I am out to set upon you,' or stick to mathematics, where you can be true.

Russell at the time found this powerful, but years later he wrote:

I find it difficult now to understand the devastation effect that this letter had upon me. I was inclined to believe that he had some insight denied to me, and when he said that my pacifism was rooted in blood-lust I supposed he must be right. For twenty-four hours I thought that I was not fit to live and contemplated committing suicide.

Perhaps part of the explanation of this extraordinary effect is the natural assumption that what is expressed with great vehemence must be based upon something, or else is stark mad: and Lawrence, though odd, was not stark mad. And there was just enough plausibility in what Lawrence wrote to stimulate Russell's angst. Russell, after all, was already somewhat in doubt as to whether his rationalist outlook on life was sufficient.

No man can be fully rational in the sense in which Russell once implied, namely someone the strength of whose belief in something is proportionate to the strength of the evidence in its favour. We all of us resign to others the right and duty to ascertain the strength of the evidence in favour of a proposition that we shall never, and never could, ascertain for ourselves. Many, probably most, of the things that we believe, for example that physical objects are made up of atoms and molecules, are quite beyond our powers to prove. I doubt that one man in a thousand could prove that the blood circulated in the body, but I doubt that one man in a thousand would deny it. The believers would no doubt say that someone had proved it in the past and could do so again if necessary. But in essence, this leaves most of us most of the time in the position of believers in authorities: we believe something because we trust the people who say it is so.

In other words, few of us can do without authority for much of what we believe. When I say that I believe that the European cuckoo flies southward each year to Equatorial Africa, I believe it because of the facts adduced by those in which veracity I also believe. There is a whole hinterland of faith to my belief that the cuckoo migrates, including in the system of academic certification of scientific researchers into the cuckoo's conduct.

Whoever else he may be, the rational man cannot be the person whose beliefs are held with strength proportional to the evidence in their favour. And yet the notion of the rational man is not quite without meaning.

Moreover (what is less often remarked), no one can be entirely irrational and survive. The madman who looks for water and drinks when he is thirsty is adapting his behaviour to his desire in a rational fashion. Much of what he does may be indistinguishable in its rationality from the behaviour of the sane man. Total irrationality is probably as difficult to maintain as total rationality.

As with all continua, the dividing line between the rational and the irrational man is not precise, among other reasons because there are so many things for a man to be rational about. A man may be rational about one thing and irrational about another. Aware of the difficulty of defining the rational man, perhaps, Russell might have succumbed briefly to the opposite temptation and supposed that if there cannot be total rationality, then there might be wisdom in irrationality. This was Lawrence's view. He wrote in one letter to Russell:

> One lives, knows and has one's being in the blood,
> without any reference to the nerves and brain. My blood
> knowing is overwhelming. We should realize that we
> have a blood-being, a blood-consciousness.

As Russell remarks — the Russell of 1956, that is —
Lawrence's views, if taken seriously, lead straight to
Auschwitz. Incidentally, the fact that Russell refers to
Auschwitz, implying that it is the worst of horrors imaginable,
suggests that those horrors of the Holocaust did not need to
be rediscovered after a lapse between the end of the war and
the release of Stephen Spielberg's film, as is sometimes alleged.

Clearly, Lawrence's charisma did not depend upon his
capacity for discussion. As a thinker, he was far worse than
merely nugatory, whatever his merits as a poet and novelist. I
suspect that the intensity of his visage, his burning faith in the
truth of what he was saying, and the extremity of his opinions
were what caused people as clever as Russell to fall under his
spell (albeit briefly). And who would like to say that his own
critical faculties could never be abrogated by such charisma?

The idea that Russell's opposition to the war was but
mirror-image blood-lust was simply ridiculous, laughable in
fact. But then Lawrence didn't have a very lively sense of the
ridiculous. Charisma and the absurd are often
interdependent.

Having spent so much of my life reading, I am always
surprised (and not a little alarmed) to discover how much I do
not remember of what I have read: worse, it seems to have left

no trace on my mind whatsoever. When I was young, I had an almost photographic memory for tables of figures, but either the camera or the film on which images are inscribed has deteriorated severely (there are probably whole generations now who do not know what camera film is, or was, and have no experience of the struggles we had to change rolls of film without exposing them to light). My memory for text, however, was never very strong. Nevertheless, wanting to believe that I have not entirely wasted so much of my life entirely on books, I try to believe that everything I have read has contributed some small ingredient to the melting pot of my mind. It is perhaps because my memory is so unexceptional that, when people ask me what books have influenced me most, I have great difficulty in replying. If only I could answer with certitude, Jane Austen or Schopenhauer.

What is more surprising to me even than my lack of recollection of what I have read (sometimes I have forgotten even *that* I have read it!) is the same lack of recollection of having visited exhibitions whose catalogues I have bought. I know that I have visited the exhibitions of those catalogues because I never buy catalogues of exhibitions I have not visited. Again, I hope that the forgotten experience added something to the rich mix of my reflections, but of course it is impossible to decide the matter either way because no controlled experiment can be done to decide it.

Yesterday I was looking through my collection of catalogues and came across a slim volume titled *art behind the wire* (artful absence of capitalisation being that of the publishers, not mine). It had been published to accompany an exhibition in the Walker Art Gallery in Liverpool in 2004, and it is alarming to think that, though I must have attended it, I would have been prepared to swear in court that I had not.

The exhibition, a very small one, was of art produced by German refugees to Britain who were interned as enemy aliens in a camp in Liverpool in 1940-41. Many of them were subsequently sent to a camp in the Isle of Man, before officialdom realised that refugees from Nazi Germany were most unlikely to want to assist the German war effort but rather more likely to want to assist the British war effort. Perhaps it was only to be expected that, in the dire situation of the time, paranoia about a fifth column should have seized the government: the German Hospital in Dalston, London, founded in 1845 to treat German-speaking residents of the city (of whom there were tens of thousands) by German-speaking physicians and surgeons, including the great Sir James Paget who first described the two diseases that now bear his name, ceased in 1940 to have any German connection and became an ordinary hospital because it was feared that patients were signalling to the overflying Luftwaffe from the flat roof of the 1930s Art Deco annexe to the main hospital.

I learnt quite a lot from reading this slender volume, for example that 27,000 of the roughly 70,000 German immigrants to Britain were interned during the war at some time or other, and that internment came to an end when public opinion turned against it when 600 of 1200 internees who were being transported by ship to Australia were lost when the ship was torpedoed by the Germans.

At first the conditions in the internment camp at Huyton, Liverpool, were very poor, though more from disorganisation than deliberate cruelty or neglect, the former being characteristic of British administration. While the effects of disorganisation and cruelty may be indistinguishable, amelioration is more likely in the case of the former, and conditions did improve in Huyton, none of the inmates of that camp making the mistake of thinking that things were no better in England at the time than in Germany. A local politician, Eleanor Rathbone, visited the camp, and her visit alone brought succour to the inmates.

Among the latter were a couple of artists, Walter Nessler and Hugo Dachinger. The latter's work in particular was impressive. In the absence of professional materials, he used whatever came to hand, as did the inmates of lunatic asylums in the past: and it is said that on one occasion he made a paintbrush of his own hair. Some of his work was painted on sheets of newsprint, at first forbidden to internees but given to him by the guards. His watercolours on newsprint were easily mistaken for innovative modernist work in a freely chosen medium. The watercolour on one such piece of newsprint, on which the news of the war was all bad, had but one piece of good news: 'Boys' increased gain in weight' — at a time when gain in weight still signalled improved rather than worsened health. Dachinger's watercolours of the camp would make anyone who did not know that they were of Liverpool might think that they were of Dachau, but shortly after his release from the camp, which was closed, an exhibition in London of his work during his internment was held to great acclaim. Such a thing, of course, would have been unthinkable in the Germany of the time.

Dachinger's work bears some resemblance to that of George Grosz, and its impact is almost as great. It is all the more surprising, then, that I have no recollection of having seen it, and the book came to me as if to a tabula rasa. What makes it even more surprising is that I have a slight family connection to the internment of what some internees called ironically, but also literally, *His Majesty's Most Loyal Enemy Aliens*.

My mother arrived in England in January, 1939 aged 19, and her cousin, Celia, two years younger, arrived a couple of months later. Celia, but not my mother, was interned briefly on the Isle of Man in 1940. I never found out exactly why this distinction was made between them, for my mother was considered for internment, the major who interviewed her deciding that it was not necessary. Perhaps it was because she had learned to speak accentless English, which Celia, despite her perfect command as far as grammar and vocabulary were concerned, never did (she even published some poetry in English). If anything, of course, this might have made my mother more dangerous than Celia, if either or both were a spy for the Nazis, because no one would have recognised my mother as German; but the official mind has never been strong on logic or good sense. Celia once told me that she spoke the German of a fifteen year-old girl, but after the war she served as an interpreter for the American army, working with one Henry Kissinger (whether this was true I never investigated). Certainly, when she lived in Paris as a bohemian before she married a German refugee to Australia who made a lot of money from chocolates, she was later the mistress of the black American writer, Richard Wright, for a time.

I did not know Celia very well, but I would see her in Paris from time to time on her prolonged visits from Melbourne.

She had a contempt for Australia, which I never had: in fact I see it as a place of romance. She told me that she had enjoyed herself greatly in the internment camp on the Isle of Man. I did not ask her how or why, but she being a very beautiful woman I suspected at least one answer, but I very much regret that I did not show more curiosity about her experiences. The past is not only another country where they do things differently, but it is irrecoverable the moment we cease to enquire about it.

Looking at *art behind the wire*, I realised how much of my life is now a black hole, even for me. In the course of my journalistic career, I have sometimes scribbled notes in a little notebook preparatory to writing an article, but the notes are now completely incomprehensible to me. Worse still, they often refer to matters that one might have thought were unforgettable, such as interviews with ex-prisoners in Georgia in the ex-Soviet Union, who were horribly tortured: but I search my mind in vain for any real recollection of them.

Is my black hole of a life unique or unusual, or is it the universal human condition?

Returning briefly to the lecture that I gave to the Bridgnorth Historical Society on the life and work of the Reverend George Bellett, I found a passage in his memoir that he wrote for private circulation, and which was continued by his daughter, that brought a strange association to mind. The passage is by his daughter, whose death was commemorated with a brass plaque in St Leonard's church, though she had moved away from the town fifty years before. This, surely, is testimony to the lasting memory that Bellett left in Bridgnorth after he left in 1871, having served thirty-five years as incumbent. During that time, he preached more than a thousand sermons, each one written down beforehand; and if the three sermons of his in my possession that are printed are typical of their length, it means that he wrote the equivalent of 10,000 printed pages of sermons, that is to say, thirty or forty normal books. This is unimaginable today.

Perhaps unsurprisingly for a nineteenth-century clergyman, Bellett was very keen on Divine Mercy and Providence as an explanatory principle. He attributed the end of the cholera epidemic that struck the town in 1849, for instance, to God's mercy brought about by the day of humiliation and prayer that he organised (with the permission of his bishop) on which the shops shut and the streets emptied, unlike (as he lamented) on Sundays, when some light-minded people tried to amuse themselves on their day of rest. By the time of the day of humiliation and prayer, in fact, the epidemic, in which 69 people of the town died, had burned itself out.

Whenever anyone known to him closely recovered from a serious illness — his wife from smallpox, for example — he wrote of Divine Providence, though one might have thought that Divine Providence could have saved itself some trouble by intervening earlier in the chain of causation and preventing the disease in the first place. Bellett never lost his faith in the fundamental goodness, justice and mercy of whatever happened: when in late old age he fell and injured his face, he thanked God (literally, not figuratively) for His mercy in ensuring that his injuries were not worse. Whatever one may think of this as philosophy, it has obvious psychological advantages for him who believes it, advantages of which we (I mean modern irreligious man) know nothing. The advantages follow faith, not the other way round.

The passage that struck me so forcibly was another paean to Divine Providence and Mercy. In it, Bellett's daughter (who never married) recounts the travelling wild beasts' show that came to Bridgnorth during her childhood:

> Our father took us and entered fully into our enjoyment of seeing the different animals. As a conclusion of the exhibition, a woman was to go into the leopards' cage and make the animals go through some performance. She was evidently frightened at the part she had to take, and the manager was angry and still insisted on the promised programme being carried out; in the midst of their dispute, they both went into their cage, and in the heat of their tempers left the cage door a little ajar; one of the leopards saw this and made a spring at it, most mercifully the man had just time to close it with his foot or the creature would have been out amongst us, the consequences of which would have been so awful that my dear father could never recall the scene without an expression of God's overruling Providence.

This again strikes the non-religious person as rather absurd. Why did Divine Providence leave it so late in the day to intervene when the whole problem could have been averted from the first? To this, I suppose, the religious person would reply that God allows things to go on as long as they did to keep us on our spiritual toes, as it were, and to teach, or remind us, that we should not take our lives for granted, but be ever grateful for their existence and continuation. This seems to me to be nonsense, but it makes better people of those who believe it, because those who take everything for granted are often embittered by reversals and are seldom very attractive. In fact, the Reverend Bellett, in one of his published sermons preached in 1851 (he preached his last sermon at the age of 88, despite being nearly blind and deaf), put it rather well, in meditating on a passage from the *Book of Job*, 'He giveth no account of any of his matters.'

> This passage of holy scripture has often comforted the mind of a Christian, when reflecting on some of God's providence, which he is at a loss to understand. Difficulties of this nature occur very frequently, Events take place, the meaning of which we cannot unravel, and respecting which we can form no probable conjecture, as to what God's purpose is in bringing them about... It quiets the mind under such perplexities to learn, that it is the will of God that we should meet difficulties that we cannot solve.

Yet again this strikes the non-believer as odd: the belief in Divine Providence obviously preceding the evidence in favour of its existence. And if all that happens is in accord with Divine Providence, what does it matter how we behave, since all that we do will be equally providential? This is similar to the problem of revolutionary activity posed by Marxism: if revolution is inevitable anyway, who should I do anything to help bring it about unless, *per impossibile*, to think of myself as an agent but rather as a vector of forces over which I have no control.

Of course, there could be no wild beasts' show today in Bridgnorth (except of the metaphorical kind to be found in the pubs on a Saturday night): Health and Safety would not permit it, as much for the sake of the beasts as for that of the audience. But a few years ago, in the small town called Les Vans in the Ardèche, in France, where I have a house, a German couple came with a travelling exhibition of reptiles. It was held in the town's *Salles des fêtes*, to a small audience. The reptiles on display increased in size as the show went on, the penultimate exhibit being a Burmese python of impressive length and girth, probably fed on frozen rats, and the last being an alligator. I suppose that the authorities permitted the exhibition because they considered that reptiles are too small-brained as a zoological order to suffer much or be humiliated by a gratuitous display of themselves. At any rate, the children in the audience were enthralled, as (I am slightly ashamed to admit) was I. I do not *like* reptiles but am fascinated by them. Amphibians, on the other hand, I both like and find fascinating.

I found the show oddly reassuring as well, in that there was still a possibility of a life such as the German couple led. Whatever the discomforts and financial insecurity of a life taking their reptile show from small town to small town, living in a camper van with a menagerie of cold-blooded creatures, one or two of which might be dangerous, they were free in a way in which very few of us nowadays are free. They reminded me of Sissy Jupe, in Dickens' *Hard Times*, the circus girl who knows better how to live than all the Gradgrinds and

Bounderbys of the world. I admired and even envied them, and if I had been much younger might have asked them to take me with them. What became of them, I wonder?

The only time I have been to prison as a prisoner (and then only for an hour or two) was in Albania, but it was long enough to hear a man being beaten by the police. His cries of pain still ring in my ears if I think of it. Fatos Lubonja was in prison in Albania for approximately 75,000 times longer than I.

He was arrested at the age of 23 having written disobliging things about Albania's monstrous dictator, Enver Hoxha, in a private diary — not that the regime recognised any such category as private. His father had been a close associate of Enver Hoxha (a very dangerous thing in the long run to have been) but disagreed with him about the break with the Soviet Union, which drove Albania for a time into the welcoming arms of China before Hoxha broke with the Chinese also and became, in his own opinion, the only genuine Marxist leader in the world.

In every country, there was a groupuscule who believed him. I knew a bookseller in Birmingham who believed him and tried to sell volumes of his memoirs to West Indian ladies who wanted Bibles.

Once someone became Hoxha's enemy, at least in Hoxha's mind (in which suspicion grew like Japanese knotweed), his relatives became enemies by association, hence the search through Fatos Lubonja's diary. An initial sentence of seven years was prolonged by twenty, and if the regime had not been overthrown, he probably would have been in prison still. Had he died in prison, his remains would not have been returned to his family until his whole sentence had been served. Mere death was not punishment enough for the dictator.

In his first book translated into English, *Second Sentence: Inside the Albanian Gulag*, Fatos Lubonja relates his re-arrest while he was already in prison and his trial for allegedly belonging to a group (a complete figment of the imagination of the Sigurimi, Albania's version of the Stasi or Securitate) dedicated to the overthrow of the regime. Three of his co-accused were shot, one of them being his best friend who, unlike him, was a believing communist. The climax of the book is the sadistic way in which the author was shown photographs of the executed men after execution, with the implication that he could easily be next. His best friend had also been beaten before being shot.

In *Like a Prisoner: Stories of Endurance*, Lubonja recounts the lives of some of the prisoners with whom he shared his seventeen years in various prison camps — that is to say, the prison camps within the vast prison camp that was Albania. (When I visited the country for the first time, under Hoxha's successor as dictator, Ramiz Alia, there was only one flight a week to the outside world; the entire coast was swept with searchlights to reveal anyone trying to escape their happy lives in the country, the attempt being regarded as treason, and there were spikes to impale parachutists pointing up from every post in every vineyard.)

Conditions in the prison camps were atrocious, of course, such that one began to feel ashamed on reading of them of one's inclination to complain bitterly of what, after all, are but minor inconveniences that do not even rise to the level of hardship: not that such temporary feelings of shame will prevent further bitter complaint over minor inconveniences in the future. Complaint is never, and perhaps can never be, strictly proportional to its occasion.

Inevitably, one wonders how much of one's own humanity would have survived in conditions such as those of the Albanian prison camps: it is difficult to escape altogether the idea that it is only under the severest test that one discovers who one truly is, of what one is truly made. Good fortune is as much a test of character as bad, no doubt, but to survive it with flying colours does not confer quite the same kudos as having survived the worst ill-fortune.

Fatos Lubonja's sketches of human character under the severest test possible are what is often called unforgettable, but few of us long remember all that we read, and fewer still are those that keep it in mind. Be that as it may, Lubonja makes clear that human variation is not extinguished even in the direst of conditions, and I suppose that is a consolation of a kind, even if the worst conditions often bring out the worst in some people. The worst, of course, is very bad indeed.

But, perhaps surprisingly, there is good also, and finer feeling: not that they guarantee a happy ending. The case of Navi, for example, is instructive. He was sent to Czechoslovakia in the early days of the Albanian communist regime to learn medicine, and there he fell in love with a Czech girl called Vlasta. They swore eternal love and promised to be true to one another when he was recalled to Albania after the break with the Soviet Union. Navi was driven by his love of Vlasta to try to escape from Albania but was caught and remained in prison camps for nearly thirty years.

During that time, he received only one letter from Vlasta and as he himself recognised, it was inevitable that she should marry someone else. Navi then lavished his love on a cat, and there is no better description anywhere[6] of the intense love a man can have for an animal, or of the balm to a wounded soul that an animal can provide, than in this book. But someone with a grudge against Navi — who was the camp doctor as well as prisoner — drowned the cat, causing Navi the intensest grief.

Eventually, with the downfall of the regime, Navi was released and went to Prague to meet Vlasta. They became deeply attached to one another again, without in the process annoying Vlasta's husband. Navi found a medical job in Prague (where, remember, he had qualified as a doctor), but the story does not have a happy, let alone a sentimental, ending. Five years after his arrival in Prague, Navi jumped to his death from the fifth floor of his hospital. One can imagine the reasons: but in any case, the story is a corrective to the shallow idea that for every human tragedy there is an equal and opposite means of overcoming misery that has been endured. A life laid waste is a life laid waste, and remains so.

In another story, equally tragic, a man who is sustained during his captivity by the composition in his head of poems which he hopes one day on his release to publish (much as Solzhenitsyn memorised his work while in the Gulag) is so brain-damaged by the time of his release that all memory of his poems is gone, and he is able to write down nothing more

---

[6] Except, perhaps, in Turgenev's story, *Mumu*.

than his initials.

There is a powerful parable of religious faith in this book. One of the camps in which Lubonja is held has its Don Quixote, a man who believes against all reason that an amnesty for the prisoners is about to be announced on the next national holiday. No number of disappointments ever disillusions him: he always has an explanation for why the amnesty was not proclaimed as he had foretold, for example that the dictator was distracted from it by more pressing matters, and that the amnesty will be proclaimed on the *next* national holiday instead. He does not, or cannot, believe that the dictator is anything but well-intentioned, as a Christian believes in the goodness of God despite the manifest evil in the world, and therefore that the non-proclamation of the amnesty is never his fault. And strangely enough, the Don Quixote of the camps converts others to his view, and even the author himself comes half to believe him. Conviction is often mistaken for evidence.

He is an absurd figure, this Don Quixote of the camps, but we come to love and even admire him.

Like a Prisoner is a profound meditation on human nature, on the simultaneous human desire to accommodate and not to accommodate to the circumstances in which humans find themselves against their will.

The first poet to whom I ever spoke was (I think) Dannie Abse. I may briefly have spoken to Wendy Cope or Fleur Adcock after a poetry reading, but I cannot be sure of the dates. At any rate, Dannie Abse was the first poet with whom I actually *conversed* a little.

I had read nothing of his poetry: it was his status both as doctor *and* poet that impressed me, as Silas Wegg was the literary man *with* a wooden leg in *Our Mutual Friend*. I, too, was a doctor, just about, and I too aspired to write. How much I must have bored poor Dr Abse with my earnestness, my egotism, and my ignorance! He put up with it all very well, at least as I remember: perhaps he displayed signs of boredom or exasperation that I was too self-absorbed to have noticed. I blush to think back on my easy assumption of equality with him, not recognising the great gulf in distinction between us.

I met him again many years later, when he was in his nineties. I was a judge of the Hippocrates Poetry Prize, of which he was a patron, and there was a dinner in the Athenaeum given by Professor Donald Singer, one of the two founders of the prize.[7]

The prize was for a poem written by any worker in health care. Donald was a distinguished physician, a highly accomplished and cultivated man, cosmopolitan and with wide interests. He exuded philosophic even-temperedness and unruffled good humour; he spoke in a way both to calm the furious and alert the somnolent. He had the faintest of Scottish burr in his speech. He was slim, elegant in an understated way, and was the last man, one would have thought, to have a heart attack.

He had a heart attack, and a fatal one. He collapsed on a golf course and was kept alive by the retired police inspector with whom he was playing, but the ambulance took an

---

[7] The other was Professor Michael Hulse.

eternity to arrive, and he never recovered consciousness. He was younger, fitter, more careful of his health than I (there is no justice in the world), and I still find it difficult to believe that I shall hear his distinctive, reassuring voice no more, or see his gentle but intelligent smile.

I had never judged anything for a prize before and found the judgment of poetry far from easy. We were three judges, and soon found ourselves haggling like carpet salesmen in a souk. All the entries were anonymous, of course, and perhaps astonishingly we alighted on a poem by an American doctor whose poetry was already well-known and highly-regarded. We felt as pleased for ourselves as for him.

Dannie Abse was a guest at the Hippocrates Prizegiving ceremony, being, perhaps, the most eminent doctor-poet of the English-speaking world. In his nineties, he seemed very spry, certainly with no mental diminishment. He enjoyed himself and was a cause of enjoyment in others. His manner was modest, completely free of the arrogance of a sense of achievement or of the awareness that he was the most distinguished person present. He died three months later. Frailty, thy name is old age!

Abse's wife, an art historian, had been killed in a car crash in the year 2000 in which he had been the driver, and he now had a companion considerably younger than he. This was not a betrayal of the memory of his wife — there was no rational argument against it, and no possible moral condemnation of it — and yet I felt that I could not have done the same in the circumstances. But people are different and in any case you cannot tell how you will react to circumstances until you are in them.

Abse wrote a diary and a book of reflections during the year following the crash in which his wife of fifty years was killed instantly. He had been slowing down to leave a motorway when a young woman, who had fallen asleep at the wheel, collided with their car at seventy miles an hour. Abse sustained relatively minor injuries — broken ribs, cuts to his face — but his wife was killed instantly. The young woman responsible wandered distractedly at the scene of the crash, saying 'I'm sorry, I'm sorry!' Abse, mildly confused, refused treatment at first and told the ambulance men to go away.

A friend of mine, of exactly my age, had an accident (entirely his fault) in which he ran into the car in front of him. Briefly unconscious, he insisted to the police that he was perfectly all right. Fortunately, his wife, who had not been in the accident, arrived and ordered him to hospital. She had an authority over him that the police had not.

The young woman who killed Mrs Abse received a light sentence: a fine of £1200 and the withdrawal of her licence for a year. My friend had a similar sentence and, living in a rural area, had to be chauffeured around for a year. I should be delighted to be relieved of the burden of driving myself, but not at the cost of an accident. If I had been Abse, I should have oscillated between outrage at the lightness of the sentence and recognition that greater severity would have been pointless and even sadistic. The young woman was clearly not malicious and no doubt suffered greatly for what she had inadvertently done. But it is difficult to align one's feelings with one's rational thoughts.

Again, I do not think I could have done what Abse did after the accident: write a diary. I am sure it was therapeutic for him to do so, and indeed I once advised a friend of mine who had been raped and nearly murdered to do the same. It was certainly therapeutic in her case and helped her to overcome her anger at the police incompetence in failing to find the culprit though she was able not only to name him but tell them where he lived. Yet I do not think I could follow my own advice: as la Rochefoucauld said, it is easier to give good advice than to take it.

After such an accident, I do not think I would ever be able to laugh again, but in his book written after his wife's death, *The Presence*, Abse tells amusing stories against himself. Once, for example, he was very pleased by the reception, a mixture of joy and relief, that he received on arriving at a literary festival. He had never felt so admired. But he soon discovered that it was not for his poetry that he was so eagerly awaited: an Iranian poet at the same festival had severe gastritis and Abse, still a practising doctor, could write a prescription for him. Abse was not in the least offended; he was an amiable man.

At another poetry reading, the woman at the door wouldn't let him in without the admission fee. He told her that he was Dannie Abse, the poet who was giving the reading, but she wouldn't believe him because he looked so ordinary. The impasse was solved by a tipsy man in the queue behind Abse when he shouted, 'Let the bugger in!'

Abse was free of the conceit of authors. Poets may be the unacknowledged legislators of the world, but they have a tendency to acknowledge themselves as such.

At the end of the book, there is poem to the memory of his wife with the lines:

> She is everywhere and nowhere
> now that I am less than one.

Forty-five years earlier, in 1952, in a book of poems titled *Walking Under Water*, there is an *Epithalamion*, a poem to celebrate a marriage. In it, there is the line:

> We, more than one, less than two…

Abse was very disparaging about his own first two books of poetry, mentioning that Walter Hutchinson, the managing director of the company that published them, committed suicide shortly afterwards, playfully implying some kind of causative relationship. Of course, there was none. Abse's first book was published in 1948, the second in 1952, and Walter Hutchinson committed suicide in 1950.

I think, though, that Abse's self-deprecation was genuine, though self-deprecation can sometimes be difficult to distinguish from self-praise. Be that as it may, I found *Walking Under Water* a fine book, not to be deprecated.

Impossible is a short novel — or novella — by the Italian writer, Erri De Luca. It has the same title in English and French but in Italian it is *Impossibile*, which makes me wonder what Sam Goldwyn would have said if Italian rather than English had become the language of America: *in tre parole, im possib ile*, perhaps.

The plot of *Impossible* is simple enough. It consists of an enquiry carried out by an Italian examining magistrate on a man much older than himself who is suspected of having thrown a man to his death in the Dolomites. Both victim and suspect were members of an armed revolutionary group in the 1970s, in what the Italians call the Years of Lead. Once close friends, the dead man turned state's evidence and informed on his former associates. The examining magistrate does not believe that the two men found themselves in a remote part of the Dolomites on the same day, on the same track, by coincidence; he believes that the suspect lured him there on order to carry out an act of vengeance. The suspect maintains, on the contrary, that it was pure coincidence that they were in the same place at the same time, and though they had had no relations since the suspect was released from prison, they were both enthusiasts for mountain walks. He says that the victim was walking ahead of him, disappeared from view, and fell from the path to his death. He was not pushed, as the examining magistrate suggests.

The evidence against the suspect is purely circumstantial. First there is the fact that they were in the same remote place at the same time; second that there was a clear possible motive, revenge. Third, he had the opportunity; fourth, there was no other suspect, and no other witnesses.

The suspect points out that, when he realised that the deceased had fallen, he at once called the emergency services on his mobile phone: but the examining magistrate is easily able to explain that away: he called the emergency services precisely to divert suspicion.

The book consists largely of the transcript of the examination. In the end, for lack of evidence, the suspect has to be released, which the examining magistrate experiences as a defeat. He seems to have none of the duties of the prosecutor in an English trial to be fair, at least in theory, to the defendant and not to secure a conviction at all costs.

Erri De Luca was himself a member of *Lotta Continua*, the violent far-left Italian movement of the 1970s. He is a keen walker in the mountains. He has experienced interrogation by investigating magistrates himself. The book therefore has an air of partial autobiography.

What surprised me about the examining magistrate's method of questioning was its looseness, its straying from the central question: did the victim fall or was he pushed? It might be true that the two men found themselves in the same place at the same time by coincidence, and it might be true that the victim fell to his death: people do sometimes fall to their deaths from narrow mountain paths, to say nothing of suicide. The examining magistrate's explanation of the suspect's call to the emergency services was plausible enough, but plausibility is not proof, besides which a failure to call them would have been just as suspect — so according to the magistrate's logic, the suspect was damned if he did and damned if he didn't. The fact is that many or most actions are capable of more than one interpretation, and once one has decided that a person is guilty, all his actions go to prove it. A kind act by a man whom one believes to be a swine can easily be interpreted as an attempt to deceive or mitigate.

The magistrate finds even the suspect's liking for solitary walks in the mountains suspect. Surely there must be an ulterior motive behind it? No doubt it is an elementary error to take the protagonist of a novel for the author himself, but it is difficult to believe that it is not De Luca speaking for himself when his protagonist tries to explain — very well, actually:

> Useless: that word has a value for me. In economic life in which everything rests on the binary to give and to have, on profit and utility, to go to the mountain, to climb, to scale, is an effort blessed by its uselessness. It is not useful and does not try to be.

In other words, it is an end in itself, it needs no justification, unlike the vast majority of what we do. It allows the walker a short break from justification.

De Luca's protagonist engages in a kind of philosophic, even Socratic, debate with the examining magistrate, and while he is depicted as the latter's intellectual superior, he seems to me to enunciate or at least imply some doubtful doctrines. For example, when the examining magistrate suggests that he has remained fixed in the views that led him to join the far left group, and that he has no sense of self-criticism, the suspect whom again one finds it difficult not to take for the author himself, says, 'You are not of an age to have been present at what happened at that time, and I do not hold you as a legitimate interlocutor about the events of those years.'

This is a disastrous doctrine, if generalised. It suggests that nothing can be known of past events except by personal experience, acquaintance or participation in them. What if an extermination camp commandant said the same thing? Would we not be appalled, revolted?

When the magistrate accuses the suspect of justifying his acts in the 1970s, the suspect replies with a very common argument: 'I have paid my debt [to society] without remission.'

But punishment is not an entry in a system of double-entry bookkeeping, nor is it the payment of a debt. If one must talk of debts, which I deny, it would make more sense to say that a prisoner has incurred even more debt to society, which has had to keep him at its own expense, often very considerable, during his imprisonment. Even his trial was at great expense, and he had not refunded its cost by being imprisoned. Nor can one pay a debt in advance of a crime and therefore have a subsequent right to commit it.

This is not to say, of course, that the criminal who has been punished should not be reinserted into society or should go on being punished ever afterwards. But this is different from having paid a debt.

In another passage, however, the suspect is perfectly right in his rejection of one of the magistrate's accusations, namely that he has expressed no remorse for what he did in the 1970s. Remorse, says the suspect, is a private matter. To make a demand that it should be expressed in public, and then rewarded by a remission of punishment, is a demand to be lied to or deceived, at least in many cases. To which I would add that in the worst of crimes, remorse does not weigh as a feather in the balance. One cannot say sorry for an atrocity.

The suspect also uses dubious arguments against treachery, which he regards as never justified. But treachery to a bad cause is not a vice, nor loyalty to it a virtue. He seems to believe in addition that if robbery is committed not for personal gain but to finance a cause, it is not a crime in the moral sense of the word — precisely what Stalin would have said while robbing a bank in Georgia.

But of course, I am mistaking fiction for autobiography.

Once, and only once, I went with my brother to see a science fiction film. As we came out, he asked me what I had thought of it.

'I thought it was rubbish,' I replied.

'But it was very well made,' he said.

'Well-made rubbish appals me more than badly made rubbish.'

To expend skill and even talent on what is not worth doing seems to me as near to sacrilege as a non-believing person such as I can imagine. Talent in the service of bad taste can result only in kitsch. Thus, the great skill of modern tattooists only worsens their activities.

It is only rarely that you read anything that deplores the epidemic of epidermal self-mutilation that has overtaken the western world in a comparatively few years. I pride myself that I was among the first to notice the ascent up the social scale of tattooing, from prison to university (assuming such to be an ascent), but my first interpretation of the phenomenon, that it was an attempt by the privileged or fortunate to identify with the marginalised, thereby turning it into a sign of political virtue, can no longer be true, if it ever was true. Retaining still a faint connotation of rebellion, tattooing is now so widespread that it also satisfies the herd instinct, never very far below the surface of rebellion as a mass phenomenon. Tattooing answers the desire both for individuation and conformity.

One of the arguments used by apologists of tattooing is that it is an ancient practice adopted by many cultures throughout the world and throughout history: what might be called the fifty-million-savages-can't-be-wrong argument. But highly sophisticated societies such as the Japanese have long gone in for tattooing, and Japanese tattooing is regarded as being the apogee of what I am still somewhat reluctant to call the art.

The Japanese writer, Junichiro Tanizaki (1886-1965) published a short story, *Tattooing*, in 1910. I read it because I assumed that it would praise the art, and being like most people reluctant to read what I suspect that I will disagree with or find objectionable, I forced myself to overcome my reluctance. One should not read only to reinforce, or provide further evidence for, one's prejudices.

In the Japan of 1910, as now, there was a class distinction in the prevalence of tattooing. Tanizaki says that 'even some of the Samurai' had tattoos, thereby implying that it was unusual, even frowned upon, in the upper classes of society. By contrast, firemen 'of course' were tattooed.

Tanizaki's description of a tattoo competition, in which the tattooed showed off their tattoos, exchanged criticism of them, or extolled the originality of their designs, reminded me exactly a century later of such a competition in Paris, where tattooing on a mass scale was a comparatively recent phenomenon (an article in *Libération*, a left-wing newspaper, said that the number of professional tattooers in France had risen from 400 to 4000 in ten years). Thanks to technical improvements — which demonstrate the evident fact that technical improvement is not improvement in all senses — it was now possible to cover large areas of skin with tattoos in a short time and somewhat less painfully than formerly. The results in Paris were heart-breaking: I remember in particular a strikingly pretty young woman, one of whose legs had been completely covered that day with a tattoo with which she hoped to win the prize for the 'most beautiful' tattoo of the day. She was in her early twenties and clutching a teddy bear.

Tanizaki's story concerns a tattooer called Seikichi. Originally setting out to be an artist, he is reduced to the status of a tattooer (I know someone in England who followed the same trajectory, again a century after Tanizaki's story). As such, he soon becomes famous, though he retains some artistic conscience:

> If you didn't have a physique or a skin that seduced him, you were wasting your time if you wanted to buy his services; and if by chance he agreed [to tattoo you], you had to give him *carte blanche* in the choice of design and price; and furthermore, you had to be ready to tolerate a month, two months, of the unbearable pain of his needles.

I was reminded here of Mr Madoff, the fraudulent financier who made his clients, or victims, feel privileged that he agreed to take them on, since he turned down many; and of course, he expected to be allowed to do with their money what he saw fit to do. His clients were mutilated financially rather than physically. One wonders whether part of Madoff's motivation was to humiliate his clients, to enjoy a delicious secret superiority over them.

Certainly, Seikichi is something of a sadist. 'When the

points of his needles penetrate the tissue, the majority of men groaned with pain, unable any longer to endure the martyrdom of swollen flesh encrusted with blood; and the more acute the complaint, the more vivid the illicit pleasure that, strangely, Seikichi experienced.'[8]

Seikichi dreams of one day encountering a woman of transcendent beauty whose perfect skin he can embellish with his tattoos. Finally, he catches a tantalising glimpse of such a one, glancing only her foot that emerges from a palanquin, a foot so beautiful that, though he does not see any other part of her, he concludes that she must indeed be the one he seeks. 'For an eye as practised as his, the feet of a human being express as much as a face.'

Five years later, he meets her, and she is as beautiful as her foot had suggested.

She is sent by her mistress, a geisha, to ask Seikichi to paint a design on her doublure, but the latter desires only to tattoo the woman of his dreams. He shows her a picture that he has painted that he says is a prophecy of her future life. A young woman in the picture shelters under a cherry tree and is surrounded by a pile of dead men at her feet. These are they who have sacrificed their lives for the woman's sake, as men will be willing to sacrifice their lives for the servant of the geisha if she completes her beauty by a tattoo that will be his masterpiece. To this end, he drugs her with a narcotic that was given him by a Dutch doctor, the Dutch having long been

---

[8] Masochism was also involved. David Beckham, the footballer who may well have played a part in the mass rush to self-mutilation, once said that the pain of being tattooed was one of its attractions for him.

the only westerners (until the arrival of Commodore Perry) to trade with Japan.

While she is drugged, Seikichi adorns her back with a tattoo of a spider. She wakes after he has finished, but in order that the tattoo should become fixed in its true glory, she has to take a cold bath that will be agonising for her.

'To become beautiful, I am ready to endure anything,' she says.

This is all very strange to me, even alien. Apparently, the Japanese of the time found tattoos alluring, as people in the West do now, though I find them repellent.

Does the spider, actually a tarantula with a venomous bite, signify or symbolise the destructive nature or possibilities of lust? Will men become ensnared in the spider's web of women's beauty?[9]

Strangely enough, spiders' webs were not uncommon motifs of criminals' tattoos in the time I worked as a doctor in a prison. Sometimes they had such a web tattooed over their face, shaven head and back. I found it difficult to rid myself of the idea that the attraction of tattoos had something in common with that of evil.

When it comes to political jokes, dictatorships are best. Perhaps this is because jokes under dictatorships are the most pointed, being risky, and oppression sharpens the wits. Perhaps for the same or similar reason, the greatest literature

---

[9] An expense of spirit in a waste of shame/ Is lust in action... Shakespeare, Sonnet cxxix

emerges from conditions of censorship, provided that the censorship in question is not so heavy that it crushes the life out of minds but rather stimulates the habit of thinking and speaking elliptically.

One of the joys of possessing thousands of books is that, in going through them, you find things possession of which you had altogether forgotten. The other day, for example, I came across a very slim volume in yellow cards with the title *The Joke's on Hitler*, subtitled *Underground Whispers from the Land of the Concentration Camp, collected by Count Alfred Hessenstein*. With drawings by a caricaturist called Spitz, it is very short, read in less than half an hour. It was published in England in 1939, just after the outbreak of the war. There is a brief introduction by the Count, who had not the benefit of post-war hindsight:

> The spectre of fear holds the German people in a cold, pitiless grip. The leaders fear the people, and the people fear the leaders. No man, no woman, trusts any other person, not even the friends of a lifetime. Germany is an immense fortress, round which armies on land and battleships at sea have laid a ring of iron and steel. There is no escape from that ring and, as time marches, the French and British bring ever mightier reinforcements to the front, tightening the grip.
>
> Upon this stranglehold falls the dark shadow of hunger. Pale and careworn men and women in worn-out clothes are standing in long queues in the streets of Berlin, Munich and Hamburg, eager to secure morsels of food. The huge fortress seems a tower of hunger. Silent, with spreading wings, a nightly vulture perches on its

battlement — Stalin.

But the jokes that the good Count has collected do not seem the best of their genre. Is this because humour is not the forte of the German people? Heaven forfend that we should resort to stereotypes! The best of the jokes in the little book seems to me to be the following:

> On the bank of a river sat several Nazi storm-troopers fishing.
>
> On the opposite bank sat a single angler, the Jew, Isaac Baruch. He caught one fish after another, while the Nazis did not catch one.
>
> 'How is it,' they yelled across the river, 'that you can catch so many fish, and we can't get one?'
>
> 'Very simple,' laughed the Jew. 'They see the reflection of your uniform in the water, and they don't open their mouths.'

Of course, it was under the communists that jokes flourished best. Recently I bought a collection of jokes told in communist Hungary, published by a Hungarian living in Sweden. (Could it be hazardous to tell such jokes in Hungary even now? Surely not.) My favourite Soviet joke is the following:

> A commissar is lecturing the troops, young recruits, when one of them raised his hand to ask a question.
>
> 'Yes, comrade,' says the commissar.
>
> 'Is it true, comrade commissar,' asks the recruit, 'there are more cars in America than in the Soviet Union?'

The commissar thinks for a moment and then replies:
'Yes, comrade, but we in the Soviet Union have more parking spaces.'

The political joke, apparently, also flourishes in the Arab world, where dictatorship is not unknown. Thirty-seven years ago, I read a book titled *Arab Political Humour*, by Khalid Kishtainy, from which I recall one joke (I recount it from memory): An American, a German and a Sudanese die at the same time and go to Hell, where they are allowed one telephone call home every thousand years because in life they committed one good act. The American puts ten dollars in the callbox and speaks for thirty seconds before the line cuts out. The German puts twenty marks in the callbox and likewise speaks for thirty seconds before the line cuts out. Then the Sudanese puts a piastre in the callbox and speaks for half an hour. The American and the German ask the Sudanese afterwards how it happens that they put so much money in the callbox and speak for so short a time, while he puts in next to nothing and gets to speak for so long? 'Local call,' he replies.

Perhaps the best political joke I ever heard was one told in Guatemala during the military dictatorship of General Lucas García. He was not only notoriously brutal but notoriously stupid. Realising this, he decides to become wise and so starts to read the Bible. And it so happens that the day after he has read the story of Solomon and the two women who claim a baby as theirs, two Indian peasant women come to him claiming the same thing. Lucas García turns to his aide-de-camp.

'*Teniente*,' he says, 'bring me my machete. I am going to cut the baby in two.'

'But, *mi general*, you will kill the baby!'

'Ah!' said Lucas García, turning to the aide-de-camp, 'so you're the mother!'

I can't remember when I bought *The Joke's on Hitler*: it must have been a long time ago, and very cheap. I looked up Hessenstein on the internet, and it seems that this slim volume is what he is most remembered for, at least if the internet be now the guardian of human memory. He also wrote, in 1944, a laudatory book about de Gaulle, *A Giant in an Age of Steel*, at a time when such praise was far from universally echoed in the English-speaking world; but this book is less recalled.

What I also discovered on the internet, to my surprise, on a very large site devoted to the sale of second-hand books, was that there were only three copies for sale of *The Joke's on Hitler*, the cheapest at £200 and the most expensive at £1500 (the latter in Germany). This is surely an indication of the strangeness of the compulsion to collect. The book, it seems to me, is as slender in its intrinsic worth as it is physically slender. No doubt it is comparatively rare, but rarity is not a virtue in itself. As a source of information or reflection, the book soon dries up. The price must be testimony to the public appetite for memorabilia of that epoch of history.

When the book was published, its price was the equivalent, in nominal terms, of five pence. At its cheapest, then, it has increased in nominal terms by 400,000 per cent at its cheapest, or by 3,000,000 per cent at its most expensive. Even allowing for the depreciation of money since 1939, it would have been a good investment in that year — if, that is, one could sell it at the price at which one now has to buy it.

The Sudanese joke, no doubt, will one day soon be incomprehensible. What on earth is a telephone callbox?

Knowledge, especially one's own, is always limited, ignorance infinite. Therefore, while going through books piled higgledy-piggledy at a flea-market in Paris, the owner of the stall obviously a man with no special regard for books, I came across a volume of plays by a Polish writer of whom I had never heard, Slawomir Mrozek, published in 1966. By that time, he was exiled to France, although the author's biography on the cover said that he was still living in Warsaw.

Mrozek was well-known in his day, his plays being performed in all the capitals of western Europe. As I started to read, it was clear to me that he was a practitioner of the theatre of the absurd, and actually rather a good one. As the book was on sale for only 1 euro, I felt I had little to lose financially by buying it. Inflation had not yet reached this bookstall.

Mrozek was the Polish Pinter, only better than he, partly because his plays were more obviously about something real and important, namely the nature of human freedom.

Included in the volume were three one-act plays. *On the Open Seas*, *Bertrand*, and *Striptease*. All three of them are absurdist, without direct reference to the situation in Poland, and certainly not confined to that situation. The best literature combines local and universal resonance, and I think Morzek succeeded in this difficult balancing act. While Pinter is a poet of neurosis, Mrozek is a poet of philosophy.

In *On the Open Seas*, three men, known only as the Small, the Medium and the Large, all dressed in suit and tie, are on a raft at sea after a shipwreck. There is no food left, they are hungry, and have to decide which of them is to be eaten. There is a discussion between them as to the proper method of deciding.

> THE MEDIUM: We are civilised people. Choosing by lots is an obscurantist hangover.
> THE SMALL: A crude superstition.
> THE LARGE: So. We can organise a referendum.
> THE MEDIUM: (To the Large) Not a bad idea. Do you agree to make a list with me? That would simplify matters.
> THE SMALL: Parliamentarianism has had its day...
> THE LARGE: But there's no other way. If you prefer dictatorship, I am prepared to take power.
> THE SMALL: No, no! Down with tyranny!
> THE LARGE: Free elections, then!
> THE MEDIUM: With secret ballot!... To the polling station! To the polling station!
> THE SMALL: One moment! If we really want to organise ourselves like civilised people, we cannot leave out the stage of an electoral campaign, which always precedes a real election.

This is ludicrous, of course, for the choice is of which is to be eaten.

In the election campaign, the Large and the Medium claim to be orphans and therefore, having suffered in childhood, due special consideration, in effect that the Small should be the one eaten. Absurdly, a postman swimming in the sea arrives with a telegram announcing the death of the Small's mother, so that he is now an orphan too. The question for the Large and the Medium becomes whether the postman is in collusion with the Small; but then another swimmer arrives, an old servant of the Large, whom he addresses as Count, who had previously claimed to be the son of a simple forester (a working-class, or alleged working-class, background being of great advantage in communist society, and increasingly in ours). In the meantime, however, the Small has internalised the need to sacrifice himself: he makes a speech reminiscent of that of Falstaff on the subject of honour.

> Freedom doesn't mean anything. It is only true freedom that means anything. Why? Because it is true, therefore better. But where to look for true freedom? Let us reason it out. If true freedom and ordinary freedom are not the same, then where do you find the true? It's obvious. True freedom is found only where ordinary freedom doesn't exist.

Freedom, as Engels said, is the recognition of necessity.

In *Bertrand*, an old man and his grandson go to an oculist. The old man has a gun and has come to the oculist because he wants to shoot Bertrand but does not see well enough to be able to recognise him. After considerable dialogue, in the course of which the old man tries the oculist's own spectacles, the only ones that work, the old man and his grandson decide that the oculist is Bertrand. The oculist pleads for his life:

> Wait, messieurs, there's a mistake, a tragic misunderstanding. I do not say that Bertrand is innocent.

On the contrary, he must be a politically odious person, but why me?... And what if the real Bertrand, horrible man, is staying warm at home with a glass of milk in front of him, and laughing at you? Has that never occurred to you?

Asked why he never said anything like this before, the oculist replies:

Because my eyes have been opened. I must admit that before you arrived, the idea of Bertrandism never occurred to me. But in the course of the discussion, the scales fell from my eyes. I am not Bertrand, you don't believe me, worse luck. But I can't stand the idea that I will be dead while the real Bertrand will go around making fun of you.

In seeking Bertrand, the grandfather and grandson will never run out of enemies to shoot.

The play's the thing wherein the author hopes to catch the conscience of the Party — except, of course, that the Party has no conscience.

In *Striptease*, two men separately and suddenly appear on the bare stage, having emerged through doors. One is reminded strongly of Beckett. Both of the men have been stopped on their way to a chosen address: but what stopped them?

SECOND MAN: Not easy to define. At times it seemed as if it were an enormous elephant that blocked the way. Or perhaps riots, although at first I had the impression of

a flood or picnic. With this fog…
FIRST MAN: Yes, it's misty, one can't see clearly.

One of them argues for resistance to circumstances, the other for accepting them because one's inner freedom is not compromised thereby. The First Man argues with brilliant sophistry for doing nothing:

> What is liberty? It is the freedom to choose. As long as I find myself here in the knowledge that I can leave by that door, I am free. To the contrary, the moment I have risen from my chair and left, I will have chosen, and therefore have limited my possibilities to act and lost my freedom. I will have become the slave of my exit.

The Second Man, the activist, replies that in staying, he is also making a choice: that of staying rather than of going. The First Man replies:

> False! False! False! I am here, but I can still go! While in going I exclude the possibility of staying.

One thinks of Hamlet:

> Whether 'tis nobler in the mind
> To suffer the slings and arrows of outrageous fortune
> Or to take arms against a sea of troubles
> And by opposing end them.

What would Hamlet have done in communist Poland? It

came as something of a shock to learn that Mrozek in 1953, then aged 26, called in public for the execution of Catholic priests as spies and stooges of the United States. He went into exile ten years later and wrote his plays that are allegories not only of communist society, but of our increasingly unfree times, in which the difference between totalitarian and non-totalitarian surveillance is narrowing.

When I was a very young doctor, I worked at the German Hospital in Dalston. The area had not yet become fashionable, and the hospital had not yet been converted into what are now always called *luxury apartments*, no matter how small and pokey, the opposite of luxury now being homelessness. The hospital had cut any connexion with Germans or Germany during the war, when, as I have mentioned, it was suspected, rightly or wrongly, but without convincing evidence, that the patients, many of whom must have been refugees from Nazi Germany, were signalling to the Luftwaffe from the flat roof of the 1930s Art Deco extension of the original Victorian building. But in the hospital library, there were still complete runs of 19th century German medical journals and in the doctors' sitting room (there was still such an undemocratic or hierarchical entity) was a pre-1939 Bosendorfer grand piano. For £5, I bought S. Kinnier Wilson's great two-volume work, *Neurology*, published posthumously in 1940. It was he who first described an hereditary disease, caused by a defect of copper metabolism, now known as hepatolenticular degeneration, or Wilson's Disease. Kinnier Wilson's son was an eminent Assyriologist who died, aged 101, in 2022.

While working in the hospital, I researched a little of its history. It was while doing so that I first realised how much I should have liked to spend my life in dusty archives, uncovering documents of little interest to anyone. At the entrance to the hospital was a wooden board with the names painted in gold of the early patrons and governors. The list was headed by Queen Victoria, the Prince Consort, the King of Prussia and Tsar Nicholas I. (In the 1856 annual report of the hospital, printed during or just after the Crimean War, and a copy of which I possess, the Tsar no longer appeared on the list of patrons.)

The history of the hospital was fascinating, at least to me. Strapped for cash, the committee of the hospital, chaired by His Royal Highness the Duke of Cambridge, decided to sell some of its land to the railway company that wanted to run a new line near the hospital. The physicians objected: the noise and vibrations of the passing trains would be fatal to the patients, 'especially the brain cases.' The committee prevailed, however, and there was a memorable scene as the first train went by. It was dark, and the committee and the physicians stood with their lanterns watching it. The patients, even 'the brain cases', came to no harm as a result. Is there a moral to this story?

I remember that the German Hospital, 'Supported by voluntary contributions' and 'Open 15th October, 1845 for the reception and care of natives of Germany, and others speaking the German language,' was riven by controversy from the beginning. Dr Sutro, second in command to Dr Freund as Directing Physician of the hospital, and to whose position he evidently aspired, spread rumours and complaints about the latter's conduct. Among the charges against him that I remember was that he had examined patients, including a woman, in the presence of a visitor, 'not a medical gentleman', and in an argument had called his Royal Highness the Duke of Cambridge 'a damned blackguard'.

Dr Freund was evidently of peppery and perhaps intemperate disposition. He repeatedly asked the Committee for more outpatient facilities, but without success. To underline his point, he called a local locksmith to unlock the hospital's holy-of-holies, the Committee Room, by far the most luxuriously appointed chamber in the hospital (as it still was in my day, with royal portraits still on the silk-lined walls), and then proceeded to examine a patient on the Committee Room table. Insolence and insubordination could go no further.

Nearly fifty years after I worked in the hospital, I came by a reprint of Dr Freund's attempted rebuttal of the charges against him. It was first printed and published in January, 1848. He admitted that he had been 'betrayed into some warmth of expression under *great provocation*' but said that if he had not admitted it from the first, the other charges against him 'would likely have fallen to the ground', having been deemed trashy and 'unworthy to occupy a Board of gentlemen for a lengthened investigation.' In other words, the insulting words used of H.R.H. weighed more in the balance than all the rest of the complaints against him combined.

These complaints were numerous. Dr Sutro complained that, against all medical etiquette, Dr Freund had interfered with Dr Sutro's treatment of a patient. Dr Freund defended himself thus (he writes of himself in the third person, perhaps to create the impression that he is objective in his own case):

> Dr. Freund, accompanied by Mr. Markovich, ['not a medical gentleman'] observed at their visits to the Hospital, from 2nd December, over the next following week, that the patient in Bed III was labouring under severe erysipelas of the right thigh, and might be benefitted by a particular step to be adopted in the treatment, to prevent mortification; and when Dr. Freund, at the end of the week, that is on Thursday, 9th December, perceived what he had long apprehended, that is *mortification*, was fast approaching, and perceiving the urgent necessity of the measure, he left a few lines for Dr. Sutro, in the hands of the House Surgeon.

Dr Sutro was morally offended by the note 'wherein Dr. Freund again seeks to interfere with one of Dr. Sutro's patients', and 'Dr. Sutro must, once and for all, forbid Dr. Freund to interfere in any way whatever.'

The 'measure' suggested by Dr. Freund was an incision to open an abscess in the thigh. Dr. Sutro claimed that this had already been done, but Dr. Freund said that the incision was not deep or long enough. According to Dr. Freund's account, his advice was eventually followed, to the great relief of the patient's suffering. This amply proved the correctness of Dr. Freund's suggestion, which, he repeated, was made for no other purpose but for the welfare of the patient, asking 'who has acted with most professional propriety on the occasion?'

The other charges against him were of extravagance — he

bought two apparatuses for the administration of ether instead of only one, defending himself by saying that it would not be easy to obtain a second quickly should the first break down, Dalston being 'so far from Town'. He also was alleged to have committed financial impropriety by inflating his expenses. As for the charge that he had been accompanied by an unauthorised visitor, he said that it was to show a third party how badly he was treated by the staff, and even to protect himself from physical attack. Was he persecuted, paranoid, or both?

From my little research, I discovered all the conflicts and dissatisfactions in the life of an institution from which we suffer today were suffered almost a century and a half before. In the first three pages of the annual report for 1856 are listed all the patrons, governors and committees of the Hospital, and there is not a single doctor among them. From the list, you wouldn't know what the institution was, or what it was for.

At the entrance to the hospital in which my mother died was a notice board on which were the names of all the most important people in the hospital, placed in order of precedence, and it was only in the fifth row that a doctor's name appeared, the medical director, and unlike the other names, his name bore no accompanying photograph.

In the year in which my father was born, 1909, John Galsworthy, who was later to win the Nobel Prize for literature, wrote a play, *The Eldest Son*, which I doubt could be successfully produced now, not because it is a bad play, for it is a good play, but because modern audiences have so lost contact with a social world other than their own that the moral atmosphere of another time would be incomprehensible and unimaginable to it: for it seems that the more multiculturalist we become in theory or ideology, the less imaginatively flexible we become. Our motto is not *other times, other ways*, but *our ways are best*, and all others are so primitive as to be of no interest to us. Starting from absolute moral relativism, we arrive at absolute moral certainty.

In the play, a member of the immemorial landed gentry, Sir William Cheshire demands of one of his young gamekeepers, Dunning (no first name is necessary), that he marry the village girl whom he had made pregnant or lose his place. A little later, however, he discovers that his eldest son, Bill, has made pregnant the daughter of the head keeper, Studdenham, and demands that Bill, as heir to the estate, *not* marry her. Thus the hypocrisy and double standards of the morality of the upper class are exposed.

Towards the end of the play, the positions are reversed. Having promised to marry Freda Studdenham, a household servant, Bill happily reneges on his promise, unlike Dunning, who decides of his own free choice to marry the village girl, having previously refused to do so, because it is the right thing to do. Thus it is not only the double standards of the upper classes that the play reveals, but the superior moral dignity of the lower orders. Old Studdenham tells his daughter that she does not have to marry Bill just because she is pregnant by him. The lower orders are more flexible than the upper, meaning that they are thereby capable of more genuinely moral thought.

This must surely have been as revolutionary, or at least as

revelatory, a departure from the conventional thought of the time as anything that Bernard Shaw wrote, and possibly it is against the common conception of Galsworthy held today, insofar as there is one, that is to say as a writer of bourgeois novels not far above the level of soap opera.

My copy of *The Eldest Son* is printed with a play that is marginally more famous, *Justice*, though I doubt that it will soon be staged again. In this play, Galsworthy inveighs (implicitly, of course, but not in very hidden fashion) against the harsh, rigid and moralistic criminal justice of his time. The play, called a tragedy, which it is, was first produced in February, 1910, when my father was ten months old, at the Duke of York's theatre in London (currently, as I write this, showing *Mother Goose*).

Justice is set in a respectable solicitor's office, father and son being both named James How. (The very idea of an old family firm of solicitors of great probity would be almost incomprehensible today, when lawyers are regarded, almost *ex officio*, as sharks.) A young clerk in the office, Willam Falder, falls in love with a woman, Ruth Honeywill, three years older than he, itself a reversal of what is conventional, who is married to a brute of a husband by whom she has two children. The husband is drunken and once tried to strangle her (as one of my patients put it, 'I've asked him not to strangle me in front of the children'). Falder and Ruth decide to run away together to South America, but they need money in order to do so, and in a moment of madness, metaphorically-speaking, Falder adds a zero to a cheque for nine pounds that he has been asked to cash at the bank, keeping the eighty-one pounds for his and Ruth's escape, though with the intention of returning the money as soon as he can. Alas for them both, he is caught and though his barrister at his trial makes a valiant effort to extenuate his crime away, arguing that he suffered from temporary but real madness, he is sentenced to three years' hard labour.

When he is released, he seeks work. Unfortunately, as soon as employers who have taken him on discover that he is a 'jailbird,' they want him no more and turf him out of their employ. His former employer, James How, agrees to take him back, but on condition that he does not see Ruth again. After all, she is a married woman and at that time her husband's ill-treatment of her was not grounds enough for a divorce. But in the scene in which Mr How is making his offer to take Falder back, the detective who first arrested Falder in Mr How's office for having forged the cheque arrives and re-arrests Falder on the charge of having forged a reference to obtain employment after his release from prison. As he is led away to inevitable further imprisonment, for Falder is guilty as accused, he throws himself down the stairs and kills himself, for he is now definitively trapped in a vicious circle of imprisonment and further crime, escapable only by the most abject poverty.

This is a powerful, if manipulative, drama, like *The Eldest Boy*, and both appeal to the generous liberal sentiments of decent people. Who could not sympathise, for example, with Ruth Honeywill in her attempt to escape her brutish, violent husband of a kind that undoubtedly existed and still exists, an attempt that the law and social convention thwarted and condemned because she was still married? And who can think of William Falder as simply a bad young man, a criminal by nature, or fail to sympathise with his efforts to find work again once he has left prison, having been branded a 'jailbird'?

Yet Galsworthy perhaps went too far in suggesting (by putting words in the mouth of the defending barrister) that criminality is overwhelmingly the result of depression caused by social conditions. This is a Rousseauvian idea contrary to the notion of Original Sin, with the corollary that if social arrangements were perfected, crime and criminality would disappear. In fact, the opposite has happened: at the time Galsworthy was writing, common crime was at an all-time, and never to be repeated, low in Britain, though the social conditions of the day, if they were reproduced today, would appal us. The destruction of the inflexible conventions of the time has not resulted in the emergence of the full beauty of the human personality but rather (here I am speculating) in the reverse. Galsworthy was not to know this, of course, and is not to be blamed: he had to deal with the evils of his time as he saw them, as we all do. Therefore, I do not reproach him for his lack of clairvoyance, and there is no doubt in my mind that he was at least partly right. Justice must be tempered by mercy, or at least understanding, and we do not want to return to the days when unmarried mothers were locked away for life, their children removed from them and blamed for the irregularity of their own birth. This was truly monstrous; but the opposite extreme, in which criminals are excused in advance, as a matter of deterministic philosophy, and mothers care nothing for the paternity of their offspring, is no better.

One small, interesting thing (to me, that is): the prison doctor in the first production of *Justice* was played by Lewis Casson, later knighted, the husband of Sybil Thorndyke, both of whom were still acting when I was a boy.

Virginia Woolf despised Arnold Bennett, but I wonder whether she also envied him. He was very popular and made a fortune that allowed him to buy a yacht. As his journal makes clear, he was a popular man who frequented the famous as an equal, and he rose from circumstances a good deal humbler than those from which Mrs Woolf rose, about which she complained with Prince-Harry levels of self-pity.

Bennett was immensely prolific. His journal ran to a million words and his journalism to at least a million more, probably several million more. He was a master of the short essay, and his work in this genre can still be read with interest, amusement and instruction. He wrote in a very clear and concise manner, but that does not mean that what he had to say was altogether trivial. He was always genial and free from snobbery, intellectual or social (his hobnobbing with the eminent was merely natural for a man who had become himself eminent), and he had a lively mind.

Consider, for example, his short essay on the decision of the Home Office not to publish the confession of a murderer on the scaffold — the death penalty by hanging was still in operation, of course, and commonly assumed to be almost a fact of nature — supposedly to spare the feelings of the relatives of the executed man. (I should add that Bennett thought the death penalty barbarous, but that was not the subject of his article). He gave his reasons for thinking that the Home Office's supposed delicacy of feeling was misplaced. I doubt that many people would have considered this subject, or many writers have written about it.

Bennett says things that are both obvious and revelatory, insofar as one has not thought of them before, and seem banal once expressed. The moral value of the murderer's confession before all men is immense, says Bennett. Among other things, it will help to settle the mind of, or reassure, the jury that convicted him. True, the jury convicted him as guilty beyond all reasonable doubt, but doubt does not always obey the laws of reason, and surely we all know that in human affairs there always remains an element of doubt. A confession thus preserves the jury from unjustified self-reproach (though the absence of a confession does not go to prove innocence, as Bennett acknowledges). A published confession will also allay public fears that justice has not been done and reinforces the belief that the justice system is indeed just, which is important for the maintenance of peace, which Bennett believes to be desirable. Publicity given only to errors of justice, which he does not in the least wish to decry or suppress, and never to its correctness, will create a misleading and dangerous impression. 'That justice should be public is an axiom. Surely then the vindication of justice should be public too.'

Bennett goes on to consider the feelings of the family and close friends of the person executed. 'The Home Secretary has given his opinion that the feelings of these persons ought to be spared, if there is a confession.' But, asks Bennett, which of their feelings? Should family pride, self-love, affectionate bias trump the good to the commonwealth that publication does? Moreover, if relatives have doubts about the condemned man's guilt, should they not be prevented from developing those feelings of resentment which could last the rest of their lives if their unjustified fears were not allayed? 'Is it more disadvantageous to him [the doubting relative], and to the state, that his pride should be hurt or that he should live in a permanent dissatisfaction founded upon error?'

Another possible cause for Woolf's envy, if she felt any, was that a delicious dish, the omelette Arnold Bennett, was named for him. Could one imagine a dish named for Virgina Woolf? One scarcely likes to imagine what it could be. I think it might be meagre and sour.

One of Bennett's little essays had a profound effect on my thinking. It was titled *Clothes and Men*.

At the time it was written (it was published in book form in 1926), English men's clothes were regarded as the acme of male elegance, as indisputably as Parisian fashions were regarded as the acme of female elegance. 'For men's clothes,' says Bennett, 'London is to masculine Europe what Paris is to feminine Europe. To be dressed in London is the ambition of youthful dandies from Calais to Bucharest.' And this, adds Bennett, despite the way that British tourists dressed when on the continent.

He draws a curious distinction between the way in which male and female fashions are commercialised. 'The world's greatest dressmakers advertise themselves freely in the papers... and they plant their establishments in prominent thoroughfares. But the world's greatest tailors are generally content to hide themselves with the modesty of violets in streets known only to taxi-drivers; the supreme sartorial names ... never imprint themselves in the Press.' Is this a difference attributable to that of the national characters of the French and British, or to that of men and women, or perhaps of both?

Certainly, Bennett tells us, 'we have a prejudice against the man who has any sustained interest in his dress. And we rather admire the man who will not go to the tailor's until he is dragged thither by his wife.' Of such company, I freely admit, am I. But Bennett adds, 'With this prejudice and this admiration I have no sympathy,' and he proceeds to tell us why.

Taking the extreme, the fop, he says, 'I would sooner see a fop in the street than a man whose suit ought obviously to have been burnt last year but one. The fop has at least achieved something, and is not an eyesore. He may often be an ass, but he is also an idealist, a searcher after perfection. We have none too many searchers after perfection…'

Not being a snob, Bennet goes on to say that it is not a question of money. Everyone has the capacity to look as smart as possible. He destroys in a few lines the argument that dress is purely utilitarian: in a state of civilisation it cannot be so. As to fashion, we cannot avoid it, and if we do not follow it in one thing, we will follow it in another. Bennett set me thinking about the role of convention in human existence and made me realise (what was obvious) that anti-convention is itself a convention. 'Platitudes, you will say,' says Bennett. 'They are; but it is astonishing how the most obvious platitudes are ignored by sensible persons in daily life.'

Thanks to Bennett, I realised something that was obvious. Complete carelessness in and indifference to dress is not a sign of a free spirit or of a mind fixed on higher objects, but of egotism. 'I'm not going to make an effort just to please your eye. You must accept me as I am.'

One of the most moving literary friendships known to me was that of Arnold Bennett and Pauline Smith. Smith was a young aspiring South African writer whom Bennett met in Switzerland in 1908, before the acme of his fame, and when she had published nothing. In her short memoir of her friendship with him, which she published in 1933, two years after his death, she tells a most charming story of him. They were sitting in the public rooms of the hotel after dinner, as people often did in those days (surely a civilised habit), when her partner at bridge, in a four in which Bennett was not participating, started to criticise her for her erratic play. Bennett sent her a hand-written note. '*I* know why you play badly. You are thinking of something you are trying to write.'

Despite his subsequent fame and fortune, he and she remained friends for the rest of his life (she lived another twenty-four years after his death). It was Bennett who insisted that she had talent, and it was he who guided her in her literary career, both on the writing and business side. He criticised her work until it was ready for publication and devoted an astounding amount of time and energy to doing so, considering that she was completely unknown. And the friendship seems to have been entirely platonic.

Pauline Smith was, essentially, a writer of two books, *The Little Karoo*, a slim volume of short stories, published in 1925 with an introduction by Bennett, and a novel, *The Beadle*, published in 1929. After Bennett's death, she published little or nothing, as if she required his approval before she published anything.

She was born in the Little Karoo, an area of the veldt that

was then in the Cape Colony, in 1882. He father, a Scotsman, was a doctor, the first doctor in the whole region, and among the first English-speaking settlers (the others were long-established Afrikaners). Pauline was sent away to school in Scotland when she was thirteen and never returned to South Africa to live, though she visited it twice. In those days of more difficult travel, such visits were prolonged. Her father died in 1899, at the height of the Boer War, when she was seventeen. She lived to be seventy-six, but it was her time in the Little Karoo and her memories of her father's profession that marked her for life and gave her the material for such slight immortality as she enjoys.

The Little Karoo contains eight stories of almost unbearable poignancy. It takes talent and skill to convey a way of life completely unknown to the reader, especially in a short compass, and Pauline Smith had it. Her community of Afrikaners had qualities, both good and bad, that derived from their inherited way of life, almost as an Old Testament people settling in a wilderness. They were hardy, upright, god-fearing and narrow-minded, content with very little but not above avarice either. Several of the stories deal with illness for which there was very little help (even if a doctor could be consulted, which was far from always). The material simplicity and precariousness of their lives is practically unimaginable to present-day readers, but Pauline Smith makes us feel it as if it were our own. Sometimes, I even caught myself envying the simplicity, though I knew that if I actually had to live it, I would not envy it for very long.

I remember something of the atmosphere of small town Afrikanerdom in the days before the end of apartheid. Of course, even then things had changed out of all recognition, and some of the modern world, for good or evil, had arrived on the veldt; but still, backwardness, material and moral, was evident. My friend and I stopped one evening in a small dorp[10] and found the only place to eat dinner. The meat was so tough that it was inedible: it must have been from an old beast that had been worked to death. Being still young and callow, we said that it was so inedible that we would not pay for it, but this so upset the owner and the cook — the insult to their pride, I think, worse than the financial loss — that they suggested that we take the meat down to the police station and let the duty officer decide whether it was inedible and whether, therefore, we should pay for it. This episode could have come straight from H.C. Bosman, one of South Africa's greatest writers of short stories.

The first episode in *The Little Karoo*, and perhaps the best-known, is *The Pain*. In this story, an illiterate tenant farmer of the infertile veldt called Jurian van Royen, fifty years married to Deltje, takes her to the hospital in Platkops Dorp, the nearest little town, which has just opened. The town is three days away by ox-cart. Deltje has been suffering for several months from a pain in her side that has not been cured by *Grandmother's Drops*, the only medicine known to them.

The couple are childless and have only each other, but their love is deep. Deltje can read and often reads the Bible to Jurian, who delights in it. 'No music could be more beautiful than this,' he believes. On a shelf on the wall which divides the living room from the bedroom (this wall not reaching the roof

---

[10] A dorp is a small town.

of their house) 'Deltje kept their few treasures':

> Her Bible, two cups and saucers thick and heavy, with roses like red cabbages around them, a little pink mug, with 'A Present for a Good Girl' in letters of gold on one side of the handle and a golden Crystal Palace on the other, and a red-crocheted wool mat, a black-bordered funeral card in memory of Mijnheer van de Wenter's mother [van der Wenter is the landlord], an ostrich egg, and a small box lined with blue satin and covered with rows of little shells round an inch-square mirror. This was the pride of their simple hearts, and these, after fifty years of life together, were their treasures.

Surely, Pauline Smith must have heard stories of such people from her father, if she had not met them personally. I have known Africans who, in their huts, had the same or similar treasures. At least they were not much troubled, as are we, by the need to look after superfluous possessions.

Jurian and Deltje, seventy-five and seventy respectively, arrive at the hospital, Jurian having made a 'nest' for Deltje of his ox-cart. We, the sophisticated readers, know that Deltje, who is weak and wasting away, has cancer; the hospital can do nothing for her, though she spends some days in a hospital bed separated from Jurian, a separation which they both find intolerable. At the last, Jurian takes her surreptitiously out of the hospital, the separation having been worse than the illness.

We know that Deltje will soon die and Jurian will be left on his own. Surely, he will afterwards soon die of a broken heart, though a doctor would no doubt diagnose some other cause of death. We would not wish him to live longer: if only he and Deltje could die together as they had lived together!

All the stories are similarly tragic. A man who has made his wife miserable suddenly realises as he is dying of tuberculosis how much he loves her, but he cannot express it before he dies, and therefore she can never know it. A teacher and a young woman fall in love but cannot marry. A pastor's daughter wants to marry a man who runs away to marry another woman and then returns to beg the first woman's forgiveness, hoping to marry her. He is under the illusion that his first wife, who has run away from him, has died, but she has not. Discovering this, he realises that he cannot marry the first woman after all.

At every point in the book, happiness is thwarted; but strangely enough, the effect is consolatory rather than desolating. Strangely enough also, one senses that one is reading allegories of the author's life. Whether having written a book that is still read nearly a hundred years later is anything to set against an unhappy life, I cannot say.

Perhaps modern readers of *The Little Karoo* will bridle somewhat at the absence of black Africans in the book, but Pauline Smith was writing of the life she knew intimately, not giving it any stamp of political approval. And what she knew was the life of the poor whites of the Little Karoo, positive discrimination in favour of whom was the very foundation of the policy of apartheid.

Some time ago, I was asked to choose stories for an anthology of short stories with a medical slant, and I regret that I did not include *The Pain* in it.

Until Annie Ernaux was awarded the Nobel Prize for Literature, I confess that I had never heard of her. Suddenly, her books appeared in very large quantities in French bookshops, and I thought that perhaps I should read one. I was encouraged in my design by the fact that most of her books were very short.

Discussing it over dinner with an intellectual with whom we dine whenever we are in Paris, who used to work for the *Institut national de la statistique et des études économiques* (the National Institute of Statistics and Economic Studies), or the *Institut national de mensonge* (the National Institute of Lying) as he calls it, he advised very strongly against reading Ernaux, even as much as a page of her, because he thought her work trivial, narcissistic, self-indulgent and quite without literary merit. I did not ask the obvious question of whether he had read any of it himself. I suspect that he had not and was going by what others had told him.

Anyway, finding myself with a three-and-a-half-hour train journey ahead of me, I bought one of her many short novels on sale at the station bookstall, of a length perfectly suited to such a journey. I chose *La honte* (The Shame), because it started in a way that would surely catch the attention of most readers:

> My father tried to kill my mother early afternoon one Sunday. He was not an habitually violent man; on the contrary, the attempt came out of the blue and was neither repeated nor mentioned again. It was as though it had never happened.

There are whole countries about whose history such silences are maintained.

The book is a search for the explanation and meaning of this extraordinary event (it is a rational assumption that it had one). Ernaux therefore tries to remember her life at the time, 1952, that it happened.

Her books are what is now known as *autofiction*, that is to say some kind of melding of two genres, autobiography and fiction. This seems to me a slippery genre. To the criticism that something in the book never happened, the answer can be returned that it is a fiction; to the criticism that something in the book is implausible, the answer can be returned that it really happened. The events described are not such as to leave a public record, and so both arguments can be employed with impunity.

All the same, Ernaux's reminiscences of that time seem to me to have the ring of truth, though there is no criterion other than plausibility by which verisimilitude or its opposite can be judged.

The author was born into the petit bourgeoisie of a small town in the north-east of France. Her parents, who emerged from the industrial working class, were socially ambitious. They had risen to be the owners of a small grocery and café, and they sent the young Annie to a convent school rather than to the local state school, as did all the other parents in their part of the town. One might take the Nobel Prize as a vindication of their decision, but Ernaux is not grateful for it. What part that decision played in her subsequent success cannot be known. She might have been destined for great things wherever she was sent to school; but at any rate, she has nothing but scorn for the school to which she *was* sent: for its religious training or indoctrination, for the values it tried to inculcate, and for the conduct that it enforced.

Her parents aspired to a higher social status than their money permitted, and they never had enough to indulge in snobbish marks of distinction such as the possession of a dressing gown, taken for granted one rung up from theirs in the social scale. Their acute awareness of social gradations gave rise to much anxiety. They did not want to fall back into a lower social class but at the same time were both envious and resentful of those above their own level.

Ernaux sees all this through the eyes of a twelve-year-old child who has to learn the do's and don'ts of petit bourgeois life in a small town, as well as the code of the school to which she is sent, where she is the poorest girl. Her life is her world, indeed for her it is *the* world. Shame arises when she breaks the school's code of behaviour, sometimes without realising it, which she is in constant fear of doing. All this is etched on a very small scale, but that scale is all the child Ernaux knows, and childhood humiliation rests with one for the rest of one's life (witness Dickens). Throughout the book, she gives the various sets of rules by which she then lived, thought she was obliged to live and which seemed to her almost as ineluctable as the laws of gravity: though she learnt years later that they were in fact arbitrary, designed above all to produce conformity. Here are the rules of her convent school:

> To stand in line in the playground at the first bell, rung by a teacher in turn, go up to the classroom in silence at the second bell five minutes later

Not to put your hand on the banister of the stairs

To stand up when a mistress, a priest or the headmistress enters the classroom and stay standing until they leave, unless there is a sign inviting them to sit, and to rush to open the door for them and close it afterwards

To lower your head and eyes every time you pass in front of them in the same way as in church before the holy sacrament

Except under medical certification, prohibition of going to the toilet at any time other than breaktime. ('The afternoon of the return to school at Easter in 52, I wanted to go [to the toilet] from the beginning of the class. I held myself in, sweating, on the verge of fainting, until breaktimes, in terror of relieving myself in my knickers.')

A close friend of mine, now in his seventies, remembers the terrible shame that he felt when he was unable to control himself at school and was publicly humiliated.

Ernaux's mother was a strong Catholic, though perhaps more in observance than in belief, for in those days to be strongly Catholic was a characteristic of the bourgeoisie which she aspired to join. Her father, who did not have even his wife's utilitarian belief in the doctrine, went along with her Catholicism for the sake of a quiet life, though he was much less observant than she. In 1952, however, he took Ernaux on a winter coach-trip to Lourdes, *en route* stopping off at tourist spots, during which Ernaux discovered the comforts of hotels (running hot water, for example) and the delights of restaurant meals, though she and her father were the poorest people on the trip, the expenses almost bankrupting him. Humiliation followed humiliation: another girl of about the same age, but of higher social status, remarking disdainfully that Ernaux wears her gymslip as if she had nothing else to wear. This is reminiscent of Estrella's remark in *Great Expectations*: 'He calls knaves jacks, this boy.' Unforgettable humiliation springs eternal in, and from, childhood.

Ernaux implies that her father's sudden explosion of rage and violence was brought about by a humiliation too far, a sudden overflowing of the cup of bitterness, as it were: and, again by implication, that the humiliation was wrought by the class nature of the then-existing society, with all its ranks, prohibitions, snobberies and so forth. Ernaux has been of the far left all her life, and I understand lives still in an unfashionable district, though by now must have the means to live elsewhere.

Her close examination of shame and its lasting effects is by no means negligible, even if one does not share her fundamentally utopian idea that there is some possible social arrangement which would abolish it from the repertoire of human emotions once and for all.

Thanks to my dinner companion, I started with a strong prejudice against any book by Ernaux. It is always a pleasure to overcome a prejudice because it reassures one that one is, at least to a certain extent, a rational being.

One of the advantages of ageing — I suppose that there are not many — is that almost any book will promote associations in the mind, perhaps not always in logical fashion.

Anita Brookner's novel, *Hotel du Lac*, provokes associations in my mind. The protagonist, Edith Hope (a surname that belies her character), is a romantic novelist who writes under the pseudonym of Vanessa Wilder (another significant name), and who is escaping an embarrassing situation in England after she has scandalously betrayed a man whom she has promised to marry. She takes refuge in a hotel by a Swiss lake just as the season is ending. Now on her own, she observes the other guests at this refined establishment very closely. She agrees to marry one of them but again goes back on her word.

I thought of the only romantic novelist whom I have ever known. She was slightly senior to me when I was a very young doctor. She wrote — or said she did — two romantic novels a year under a pseudonym, as did Edith Hope of the *Hotel du Lac*. She never told me what the pseudonym was, so I never read any of her novels. She was, or affected to be, ashamed of them, and said that she wrote them only to supplement her income, and certainly she was very well and expensively dressed, unusually so for someone who had not yet reached the pinnacle of a medical career. She was in many ways a superior person and let it be known that she was undergoing psychoanalysis with Prince Masud Khan, with particular emphasis on his princely title (to which he was not entitled). Not only was she the first and only romantic novelist I had ever met, but she was the first person I ever encountered who was undergoing psychoanalysis. I was not entirely impressed by the results (if indeed they *were* the results), for it seemed to result in an obsession with the minor flux of her own inner state. Masud Khan, incidentally, was in apostolic succession to Freud himself, having been a protégé of Freud's daughter, Anna.

The second association evoked by the book was similarly frivolous and was occasioned by the little dog, Kiki, who belonged to one of the hotel's guests. The dog, upon whom its owner, Monica, lavishes love and attention for lack of human attention, one day leaves a little puddle under him which the hotel staff, with that obsequious discretion that so marks an exclusive hotel, clear it up silently. This reminded me of our beloved little dog, Ramses, who, immediately on entering the Grand Hotel in Eastbourne, celebrated by doing what in my early childhood was called *big jobs*. Fortunately, they were well-formed, and my wife managed to sweep them up before anyone noticed, the doorman's attention being fortunately distracted elsewhere. We were worried lest the hotel concluded that such episodes were habitual with Ramses, and therefore excluded him, and us with him. Such an eventuality was avoided by my wife's swift and discreet action.

I encountered Anita Brookner a few times at the *Spectator*, not that I was eminent enough to be worthy of her notice. She was a very strange looking woman, with a small and fragile body but a head so large that it looked as if it might topple her. She, too, was expensively dressed and exuded refinement like a cold front on a weather map. If she considered me at all, which is doubtful, I think she would have thought me coarse or at least crass.

Another quality that she exuded, or at least so it seemed to me, was bleakness. The subject of her novels, that bleakness, the loneliness, and the difficulties of love or even of lesser relationships, were inscribed on her face. As is well-known, it is an elementary mistake to equate a literary protagonist with his or her creator, but it is also often difficult not to do so, especially in such a case as Brookner's, when her subject matter so exactly coincided with her life. But her books nevertheless were not *autofiction*.

I cannot quite make up my mind whether her intense concentration on the minutiae of eventless lives, or lives at least lacking in dramatic events, is a case of *magnum in parvo*, greatness in small things, rather like quantum physics, or mere triviality. Her fastidiousness had something purse-lipped about it; her habit of making very fine distinctions caused me to think of those persons who move their fingers very slightly when disapproving of a noxious insect. The novelist Julian Barnes gives a portrait of her in his novel, *Elizabeth Finch*, and no doubt he intended it to be flattering (Barnes was a close friend of hers); but to me it was the portrait of an irritating person, prissy, snobbish, pedantic and superior, and not, despite her pretensions, a very deep thinker.

At the same time, and notwithstanding any possible irritation at the exquisiteness of her distinctions, I feel an instinctive sympathy for Anita Brookner. I think the distress that was the subject of her work was genuine, as was the fineness of her aesthetic judgment. She was obviously not a bad person and her faults not such as do great harm in the world, unless shared by very large numbers. She had the misfortune to live at a time when aesthetic fastidiousness such as hers found much justifiably to lament. She was Jane Austen who had wandered into the midst of an orgy — not an enviable fate.

She had admirable powers of description. When she describes the furnishings of the hotel as being the colour of veal, one knows exactly what she means. Veal is the colour of a world in which people are afraid to make an aesthetic judgment: being so neutral, it can offend no one. We have moved much further in this direction since Brookner's day (the novel was published in 1984). Recently, my wife and I went on a brief holiday to celebrate our wedding anniversary, and discovered, via the internet, that all hotel rooms are decorated similarly, a bit more or a bit less luxuriously, all the colour of veal, with splashes of blood or other equally violent colour, to make it look as if there were some individuality to the décor. As for humans in such hotels, they are like colonies of bacteria whose traces can be wiped away with an alcoholic cloth. No doubt this all makes for hygiene and comfort, but the uniformity and characterlessness are disquieting.

Edith Hope is always considering such difficult questions as what to wear, whether her cardigans are too thick or too thin. In a world of war, injustice, tyranny, economic crisis, massacre and so forth, these dilemmas might seem less than compelling, but they occupy more of our thought than the deep questions of existence. Greatness in small things is preferable to smallness in great.

1984 (the year, not the book) now does not seem to me to be so very long ago, but it is a world away. Edith Hope writes long letters to her lover, David, a married man who will never leave his wife for her, so that she, Edith, will never have an entirely satisfactory or fulfilling relationship with him — like the lady with lapdog in Chekhov. But who writes long letters today? A text message will do.

I first bought a book by E. Phillips Oppenheim at a second-hand bookstall in Havana. It was very cheap, almost free, for three reasons: no one wanted it, its condition was poor, and the exchange rate was very favourable, though not as favourable as on the black — the open — market. The book was *The Battle of Basinghall Street*, and I read it, though I remember nothing of it except its hard orange cover.

Surely, no one was *really* called E. Phillips Oppenheim? It must have been a pseudonym made up to attract readers to his pulp novels that sold by the million and funded his lavish lifestyle (including, like that of Arnold Bennett, a yacht). But no, Edward Phillips Oppenheim was his real name, and it was hardly to be expected that a man with such a name should leave no trace on the world, even if that trace now largely consists of cheaply-produced books mouldering unsold on the shelves of the ever-decreasing number of second-hand bookshops. He lived from 1866 to 1946, dying in his villa in Guernsey to which he had had no access during the German occupation of the Channel Island during the war. This was probably as well for him, as he was Jewish.

After having bought and read *The Battle of Basinghall Street*, I gave no more thought to E. Phillips Oppenheim until one day, thirty years later, I saw a large photograph of a station as it had been in the 1920s. The bookstall was very prominent — books and newspapers were then to passengers what mobile telephones are now — and the books of E. Phillips Oppenheim were piled high and heavily advertised. I thought that if I ever came across one, I should buy it.

My chance came with *The Man Without Nerves*, the American edition of *The Banker*. It was published in America a year after the British edition, by a company called Triangle Books. Of the six books published by the company advertised on the rear cover, two were by Nobel Prize winners, Pearl Buck and John Steinbeck, and two others were by P.G. Wodehouse and Dorothy L. Sayers, names not unknown today, and another by Oppenheim himself. His fiction might have been pulp, but it kept distinguished company.

The fashion in his day was for characters from the upper classes, with a good leavening of the titled. Oppenheim seems to have specialised in crooked bankers, and the protagonist of *The Man Without Nerves* could have been Mr Madoff, except that the latter was only a swindler and not a murderer as well. But James Huitt, the protagonist if not the hero of the novel, is a banker, outwardly very respectable, who appropriates his clients' money (we do not learn what he does with it) and then suicides them: that is to say, he shoots them and then makes it look as if they have committed suicide. A very accomplished forger, he provides them with a suicide note in their own hand. He is in league with the totally unscrupulous Lord Millhaven.

It has long been my contention that no book is entirely without interest, or from which nothing can be learned. Of course, Oppenheimer was an entertainer, not a teacher, with no pretensions to higher purpose. And entertaining he undoubtedly was, though one might feel slightly guilty, if one had an intellectual conscience, at enjoying his obvious drivel. But if nothing else, his book published ninety years ago as I write this inevitably tells us something about how life has changed since then.

Most of the action takes place in a village forty miles from London. This small settlement is not yet a suburb of the metropolis and has not only a policeman but a police sergeant.

The English town in which I now live is perhaps fifty times the size but has no policeman, and in a sense it is a tribute to human nature that, in the absence of any police, there is so little crime there, at least so far.

Mr Huitt, the bank manager of the most punctilious habits and conduct (apart from theft and murder) is a figure of the type I remember from my childhood and youth, but who no longer exists. The bank manager was a solid, not to say stolid, citizen, an important pillar of the community, who oversaw the financial wisdom and probity of his customers. Personal credit and indebtedness were not then the principal motor of the economy, and people were expected, and expected themselves, to live within their means. I have a letter in my possession from my bank manager drawing my attention to the fact that I was overdrawn at the bank by a sum that even then was trifling, expecting me to correct matters very quickly. That was fifty-five years ago. I took his letter seriously and sinned no more.

The very idea of a bank manager, let alone as a pillar of the community, is anachronistic (indeed, the idea of pillars of the community has disappeared as well). My branch of the bank has closed; I do not know the name or position of a single person in my bank, or any other bank. It is true that some twenty-five years ago, someone from the bank visited me at home, I supposed to ask me to make good an overdraft. Not a bit of it! He asked me, on the contrary, whether I wanted a much bigger loan, and offered a very substantial one. 'Whatever for?' I asked, genuinely puzzled. 'Well,' he said, 'you might want the holiday of a lifetime.'

Luckily, I had never been in need of a holiday of a lifetime:

the very concept seemed to me a sad one. But what he was suggesting was that I indebt myself seriously for an evanescent, and presumably sybaritic, pleasure. Mr Huitt of Oppenheim's novel may have been a thief and a murderer, but he would never have suggested anything so idiotic.

Oppenheim depicts life among the English comfortable classes of the time. Though they did not enjoy many of the conveniences of today — you had to book a telephone call from Sussex to London, for example — they were in many respects much better off than people of equivalent standing today. They all had servants, for example, and they did not have to concern themselves with such boring tasks as everyday cooking or shopping or cleaning or washing and ironing. All was done for them as a matter of course, as is still the case in India, where the middle classes live much better than in the west, even if their incomes are lower. When Huitt relaxes at home, someone brings him his sherry, his meals, even his newspaper. His life is uncluttered by domestic trivia.

But there is also something profoundly depressing about the life of the comfortably off that Oppenheim depicts, I suspect with tolerable accuracy, namely its philistinism, its complete absence of artistic or intellectual interests. The golf course, the tennis court, the cricket pitch (not that I have anything against them) are the complete focus of their interest: indeed, anyone interested in anything else is suspect to them, as if they were either soft in the head or dangerous radicals, and certainly not *comme il faut*.

This regnant mediocrity depresses me, at least until I remember that intellectuals *do* habitually do more damage than all the well-behaved philistines put together.

For most of my life I did not think about the First World War, but curiously enough the further away in time it grows, the more salient it becomes, at least in my imagination. Without it I do not think that such cranks as Walter Gropius or Le Corbusier would have had the catastrophic effect that they did have. The War, the catastrophe of catastrophes, destroyed confidence in all that had gone before and made possible a belief in the rubbishy theories of these two evil geniuses, whose talent was more for propaganda and self-promotion than for architecture. Le Corbusier, incidentally, was a fascist in more than the usual name-calling way, and I find it difficult to understand how anyone could fail to see his fascist, or totalitarian, leanings in his urbanism and designs.

It is well-known that the death of a single, named individual affects us more than the deaths of large numbers of people unknown to us. When, therefore, I read of the death of a young man on the Western Front, I felt a sorrow almost as if I had known him personally, a sorrow that is almost a physical sensation in the region of the diaphragm. Such is the sensation I had when I read the little booklet of Leslie Coulson's poems, *From an Outpost*, published in 1917, the year following his death. It is 42 pages long, of which the poems occupy 34.

Coulson was 27 when he died. He had volunteered as soon as war was declared and chose to be an enlisted man rather than an officer. He was an aspiring journalist before the war and apparently published a few short stories as well as articles. He served first in the Middle East and was wounded at Gallipoli. He was shot in the chest on 7th October, 1916, leading a charge, and died a few hours later. (Would he have been saved if treated by modern methods?) The brief introduction in the booklet says:

> He was not by nature a fighter. He was gentle, affectionate, and like all sympathetic natures, shrank from inflicting pain. In every tribute of the many paid to him in the Press, his lovable personality has been specially dwelt on.

The writer of the introduction, identified only as F.R.C. (his father, also a journalist, perhaps) goes on to say:

> Much of the noblest youth and promise of England has gone out untimely into the dark.

This is not grandiloquence but the plain truth, as no doubt it would have been of the youth of France and Germany. 'If I should fall,' he wrote in one of his last letters, 'do not grieve for me. I shall be one with the wind and the flowers.' There is a sincere modesty in this, an absence of self-importance, which is not ours, and which, whatever one may think of the pointlessness of the war, is indeed noble. Although a city lad, Coulson was a passionate lover of the English countryside.

He had a presentiment, or suspicion, that death awaited him — not altogether surprisingly in the circumstances. In a poem titled *Premonition*, he describes his love affair, presumably while on leave from the front:

> As we kissed and clung in the passion

119

> Of love's first passionate spell.
> There came a shadow between us –
>   A shadow fell.

(I find the repetition of the words *passion* and *passionate* slightly jarring.) The last stanza reads:

> The blood in our lips was frozen,
>   I felt your warm arms fall;
> A shadow came between us –
>   The end of all.

He was right, of course. A happy and faithful married life that might have been theirs did not come to pass. The bitterness is clear in the denouement of another poem, *Judgment*:

> But when my blanched days of sorrow end,
> And this poor clay for funeral is drest,
> Then shall my soul to Thy Gold Gate ascend,
> Then shall my soul soar up and summon Thee
> To tell me *why*. And as Thou answerest,
> So shall I judge Thee, God, not Thou judge me.

Coulson's most famous poem was found in his pockets after he was fatally wounded. It is titled *Who Made this Law* and clearly blames not God but Man for all that has happened and been done:

> Who made the law that men should die in meadows?
> Who spoke the word that blood should splash in lanes?

Who gave it forth that gardens should be boneyards?
Who spread the hills with flesh, and blood, and brains?
Who made the Law?

This was clearly subversive of the war effort, implying as it does that those who started or cleaved to the war were to blame. It is especially poignant that someone who so loved the countryside should see it become a bloody battlefield.

Another, more famous young war poet's most celebrated poem was found in his kit after he was killed. Charles Sorley was twenty, already promoted captain: death in armies makes for swift promotion. His father was a professor of philosophy at Cambridge, and no doubt the younger Sorley would have had an academic career. When one sees his photograph, one almost weeps: his moustache is that of a still-pubescent young man.

Sorley had spent a year in Schwerin before the war, learning German. Schwerin is my favourite town in Germany, a town that escaped both bombardment during the second war and destruction by modernisation and modernism. It is both grand and intimate, having been the capital of a duchy in the days before German, or Prussian, megalomania overtook and destroyed the country. Its art gallery has the best collection of Dutch still lifes outside the Netherlands, and also the best collection of the French animal painter, Jean-Baptiste Oudry.

There is no doubt that Sorley's last poem is great enough to secure him a grain of immortality in the English-speaking world, at least insofar as a poem can secure such immortality. It is bitter and beautiful, as well as premonitory, astonishing in its maturity of expression (war makes young men grow up quickly):

> When you see millions of the mouthless dead
> Across your dreams in pale battalions go,
> Say not soft things as other men have said,
> That you'll remember. For you need not so.

You need not so because the dead are dead and cannot hear or benefit from your fine words. The last line is of a devastating finality that one feels almost in the pit of one's stomach:

>   …should you
> Perceive one face that you loved heretofore
> It is a spook. None wears the face you knew.
> Great death has made all his for evermore.

This last line written by an eternal 20-year-old is horrific but also consolatory. I cannot say exactly how.

It is generally agreed that the poetry of the Second World War was not the equal of, nor even a patch on, that of the First. I don't think that there is a poem from the second war, at least not one known to me, that is the equal of Sorley's last poem (albeit that I thought that the word 'ghost' would have been better than 'spook' in the penultimate line, spook being an ugly word).

    Among the poets of the second war was John Arlott, who

was important to me during my childhood and early adolescence, as he was the best cricket commentator on the BBC. I loved cricket in those days and with the natural unwisdom of youth thought that it was very important. How many days did I spend at Lord's Cricket Ground watching the game, when really I should have been attending to something else! I particularly liked watching county matches, when the crowd in that great stadium was small and thinly scattered in the various stands. There was something hieratic about cricket in those days, and I liked the feeling of understanding the sport's subtleties that so many people either could not or did not understand. Later, my wife had difficulty, being French, in grasping even that the two batsmen on the pitch were on the same side. As for me, I lost all interest in the game once it became brazenly commercial and the players, instead of clad in white and wearing cricketing caps, began to wear bright and vulgar primary colours and baseball caps, to sport tattoos on their arms and perform high-fives after some exploit or other on the field. But when I look back, I can quite see that the game as I remember it was doomed. There were then still matches between Gentlemen (the amateurs who played unpaid) and Players (the professionals of lower social standing who played for lucre). They were of equal prowess, even if the Gentlemen tended to play more flamboyantly. But as Gertrude says in her speech describing Ophelia's death, long it could not be: so unabashed a manifestation of class distinction could not survive in the modern, democratic age.

John Arlott had the most beautiful speaking voice with a soft Hampshire burr, of a type that has probably now disappeared with the all but universal spread in England of a kind of estuarine enunciation, ugly, inexpressive and mediocre. His descriptive powers were great and his knowledge of the sport encyclopaedic, but he was also a man of parts. Born in the lodge of Basingstoke cemetery, he became first an attendant in a mental hospital and then a policeman for fourteen years. He was early attracted to cricket and even played a little, but his first fame, or public notice, was as a poet. Later, he became a noted wine critic, and when he retired to the island of Alderney, he kept a large and excellent cellar.

His slim volume, *Period and Place*, was published in 1944 by Jonathan Cape, among the most prestigious, if not *the* most prestigious, of British publishers of the time. (Most have since become mere divisions of conglomerates.) I doubt that anyone would say of him that he was a great poet, and none of his poems has the impact of those of the great poets of the first war: but we ought not always to be comparing everything with the greatest of the great, for then we shall fail to appreciate what is nonetheless worthy of appreciation.

Arlott was not in the forces and therefore saw no action, but he could not thereby escape the war. By 1944, the ultimate outcome could hardly have been in doubt, but there was still much danger to be lived through, even by civilians, though these dangers were not Arlott's principal fear. His fear was really guilt that he was not putting his life at as much risk as the airmen whose aircraft he heard flying overhead (and Bomber Command had a fearful rate of attrition of 44 per cent in total, not that such a death rate is by itself a justification of its activities which, however, went almost unquestioned at the time).

Awake and tense in my island bed,
I heard our night-planes overhead,
Felt their growling roaring hurled
To flood my little curtained world.

The sound makes him fearful:

Not now the fear of pain and death
To make me check my trembling breath,
But guilty fear for friends who fly,
Simply to do a job or die.

Arlott *does*, however, raise the question of the morality of
bombing campaigns: by all accounts he was a man of
genuinely human feeling.

Youth went to high adventure thrilling,
Not pausing now to weigh the killing –
Flying and fighting in our name –
If blame there be, we share that blame –
Blame not purged by praise of nations
But only by those generations
Who, not needing passports, fly
Unchallenged over common sky.

The habit of future generations judging the actions of previous
generations by their own lights is inevitable, but never
(perhaps) as implacably so as in the present, when we so
joyously award the lowest marks possible to our predecessors,
the better to inflate our own glory.

I am unsure whether the ability of a line of poetry to conjure up the memory of an individual counts as a genuine or valid form of literary criticism, but Arlott's book, published five years before my birth, does so for me on quite a number of occasions. In the poem, *Cricket at Worcester, 1938*, there is a stanza that brought back to me many a day spent at Lord's during a county match:

> Like rattle of dried seeds in pods
> The warm crowd faintly clapped,
> The boys who come to watch their gods,
> The tired old men who napped.

This captures exactly the Lord's of the late nineteen-fifties: the sound of the applause was truly the rattle of dried seeds in pods, the near empty stands around the ground being the pods.

Arlott also knew the attraction of second-hand bookshops to such sad and inadequate creatures as I:

> Like a cloak hangs the bookshop smell,
>   Soothing, unique, and reminding:
> The book-collector knows its spell.
>   Subtle hints of books and binding —

He delineates the bookseller, a man who knows *about* books but not the books themselves:

> 'Blake's Poems, Sir — ah, yes, I know,

Bohn[11] did it in the old black binding,
 In '83.' Then shuffles slow
To scan his shelves, intent on finding
 This book of songs he has not heard,
With that deaf searcher's hopeful frown,
 Who knows the nightingale a bird
 With feathers grey and reddish-brown.

Great readers suppose that they are doing themselves good —
moral good, I mean — by their habit, but the evidence that
this is so is lacking. Is the best-read man the best of men? And
given the tens of millions of books that have been published,
what is it to be well-read? No one can read more than an
infinitesimal part of what has been written, and to be well-read
in one subject is necessarily to be ill-read in countless others.
Besides, if reading can do you good, surely it must also be able
to do you harm? Even now, there is something magical about
the printed page: if it is written down it must be true or have
some substance. People thus give credence to the most obvious
rubbish, and no vicious idea ever goes unpublished.

In the *Monthly Mirror* for November, 1797, there is an
intriguing article titled *Novel Reading a Cause of Female Depravity*.
The author of this brief paper signs himself only *I.*, and in
truth makes out only a very feeble case for his proposition, so
feeble in fact that one wonders whether it is meant as a satire

---

[11] Henry Bohn (1796-1884), publisher, specialising in uniform
series of books.

on the view that it puts forward.

The article is in the form of a letter to the editor, whom it begins by congratulating:

> When I first saw your publication advertised, I formed an opinion that the Mirror would resemble too many periodical works, and be nothing more than a flimsy vehicle for detailing a few *outré* fashions, silly love stories, and examining *embroidered* poetry: I never sought to look into a number, till one was accidentally put into my hand, and it is unnecessary to add, I was agreeably disappointed. As an atonement for my erroneous supposition, I beg leave publicly to thank you for so pleasurable combining MORAL EXCELLENCE with ELEGANT LITERATURE; and heartily do I wish the happiest effects for such seasonable efforts for public good.

Nothing is calculated to make the heart sink so fast as the combination of moral excellence and elegant literature, an incitement to sanctimony and boring exhortation. The supposed love of moral good often disguises the sly pleasures of disapprobation. *I.* continues:

> I now begin to hope I shall see good old days come round again — that moderately stiff stays, covered elbows, and concealed bosoms will soon be presently fashionable; and what is of far greater importance, that chastity — pure and spotless CHASTITY — will once more be the darling attribute of women. Had fashionable depravity

been confined to the higher circles of life, I should hardly have troubled you with these, my sentiments; I should have concluded it the spring of idleness and voluptuousness, and have despaired of effectually deprecating a vice which not the happy example of conjugal virtue held forth from the THRONE[12] could discountenance. But, like every other fashion, a little day hands it down to the *million*, and woman is now but another name for infamy.

Plus ça change, then: except, perhaps, for the denunciation of women that none dare utter nowadays. Also, the bad manners or habits that have been handed down to the lower orders by the higher now ascend again, only to be yet worse.

As I have mentioned, *I*'s argument is feeble and entirely anecdotal — or hardly even that, for none of the persons in his anecdotes is identifiable and might not even have existed.

Miss [the generic reader of novels] is not long in finding out "many waters cannot quench love", neither "the floods drown it"; so as Master is yet in his apprenticeship, and friends would disapprove of an early marriage, they agree to dispose of the ceremony. Nay, even when brooding over a helpless base-born infant, and surrounded by a once respectable and happy family, now dejected and dishonoured, too often does the infatuated fair one take pleasure in the misery she has created, and fancy floods sorrow *sweetly graceful*, because, forsooth, she

---

[12] George III was a model of fidelity to his wife.

is just in the same point of view as the hapless, distressed, the love-lorn Sappho, of some novel or other.

The idea that our ways of entertaining ourselves have an inevitable effect on our conduct and character is with us still, so we should not mock *I* too much, even if he meant precisely what he said, which seems to me doubtful. It is intrinsically difficult to prove what precise effect our ways of entertaining ourselves have upon us, but it would be implausible to suggest that they had no effect whatever. At the present time there is much anxiety about the influence of the social media on the mentality and even on the brain structure of those brought up on them as mother's milk.

All the same, one may be permitted to doubt whether the mere reading of novels could account for the following, supposedly the most pernicious effect of novel-reading:

> It is no uncommon thing for a young lady who has attended her dearest friend to the altar, a few months after a marriage which, perhaps, but for her, had been a happy one, to fix her affections on her friend's husband, and by artful blandishments allure him to herself. Be not staggered, moral reader, at the recital! such serpents really are in existence; such demons in the form of women are now too often to be found!

Gosh, all because of novel-reading! It must make writers proud of their power over the rest of humanity, or at least over the female half of it.

The Monthly Mirror was mainly, though not entirely, devoted to the affairs of the stage. The first article for November, 1797, was devoted to Mrs Abington, who owes her entire but tiny portion of immortality to the charming portrait of her by Sir Joshua Reynolds in the role of Prue in Congreve's *Love for Love*. Actresses in her day were both highly paid and morally deprecated, for they were supposed, almost *ex officio*, to be of easy virtue. Perhaps nothing much has changed. But Mrs Abington was not of that ilk, and the article seeks to defend her return after a period of absence from the stage:

> The event has naturally aroused public curiosity, and given occasion for calumny, the common attendant of extraordinary merit, to throw around its shafts of falsehood, and wanton in the delights of detraction.

To wanton in the delights of detraction! Which of us has not tasted of these delights?

In addition to news of the stage, there was space given to what the French call *les faits divers*, a few reported in this number of the journal:

> Seventy-five potatoes, the produce of a single set, were a few days since dug from the gardens of Mr. Scholes, of Nepsom, near Sheffield, one of which measured seventeen inches in circumference: several others were nearly as large. A crime a more horrid nature... has lately been discovered at Constantinople. A Janissary, aged 70, and his wife, were long in the practice of alluring to their house young persons whose *en bon point* suited their purpose. These they killed, and with their fat, when

boiled, composed an unguent which was sold at a high price. When discovered by the police, they were in the act of cutting up a plump Armenian of sixteen years of age. Both the miscreants, after a short interrogation, were hung up at their own door.

And also:

An alligator, of enormous size, was killed lately at Mukna Hout, in the river Houghly. The monster was basking on the beach; a two-ounce ball from a rifle barrel stunned him so completely, that he was quickly finished with a long spear: he had long infected the neighbourhood, measured twenty feet in length, and several pounds of silver and brass ornaments were found in his body.[13]

The theft of giant potatoes, boys killed for their fat, man-eating alligators: was any of it true? And what effect, whether true of false, would it have on the reader?

For those who like journalistic vitriol and excoriation of obvious idiocy, there is no one to equal H.L. Mencken (1880-1956). All journalists love an easy target — it reduces the need for thought and renders the act of writing almost an automatism — and the America of Mencken's day gave him plenty of almost unmissable targets, indeed so many that aim

---

[13] Mugger crocodiles, to which this probably refers, rarely grow to over 15 feet but killed 18 people in 2018.

was scarcely necessary. Perhaps all ages and all places are, when rightly viewed, the same in this respect.

Mencken's waspishness was famous — or infamous, I suppose — among those who were his targets. His six volumes of journalism, called *Prejudices*, are still a good read, even if some of the topical references will be lost on those who are not well-informed about the politics and culture of America from the 1910s to 1930. In the fifth series of *Prejudices*, published in 1926, at the height of the boom before the Wall Street crash, there is an *in memoriam* essay for William Jennings Bryan, one time Secretary of State and three times Democratic Party candidate for the presidency. He is now probably best remembered as the prosecuting counsel in the Scopes Monkey Trial, in which a high school teacher, Scopes, was prosecuted for having taught evolutionary theory in his high school, in defiance of the preposterous Butler Act in Tennessee, which outlawed such teaching in the state. Mencken attended the trial and wrote many reports on it, ridiculing both the prosecution itself and Bryan personally: indeed, it was he who first called it the Monkey Trial, by which name it has been known ever since. Bryan died aged 65 a few days after its conclusion, though whether the stress of the trial played any part in his death from apoplexy cannot be known for certain.

On learning that Bryan was fiercely opposed not only to Darwinism but to the teaching of evolution, most people would probably assume that he was conservative politically, even reactionary, but he was actually left wing for his time and place (the Marxists of my long-past youth were actually very anti-Darwinian).

Mencken obviously did not believe *nihil nisi bonum de mortuis*, that no ill should be spoken of the dead, or at least of the recently dead, if one had had any dealings with them. I suppose that if a man has opted for a public life, he cannot expect to be treated with kid gloves after his death — if he is treated at all. Emil Cioran says somewhere that the prospect of having a biography written of him ought to frighten any man into silence, a recognition of the fact that none of us would wish everything about him to be known.

> There was something peculiarly fitting [wrote Mencken of Bryan] about the fact that his last days were spent in a one-horse Tennessee village, and that death found him there... He liked people who sweated freely, and were not debauched by the refinements of the toilet.

Mencken called the inhabitants of the one-horse Tennessee village 'gaping primates', and though we pride ourselves on our freedom, I doubt that any modern writer would dare write this, let alone publish it in a book. The least one can say is that Mencken was no admirer of the common man, certainly not in his North American incarnation, nor was a democrat (with a small 'd'), though I am not sure that he had any better system in mind. It is always easier, and more amusing, to be against something than to be for it.

Some defenders of Bryan claimed that he was sincere, and Mencken seems to accept that sincerity is in itself a virtue and that a man is necessarily the better for being sincere. This, of course, is not so: there are few emotions more sincere than hatred and resentment, even when they are completely without justification. But in any case, according to Mencken,

Bryan was *not* sincere:

> This talk of sincerity, I confess, fatigues me. If the fellow
> was sincere, then so was P.T. Barnum. The word is
> disgraced and degraded by such use. He was, in fact, a
> charlatan, a mountebank, a zany, without shame or
> dignity. His career brought him into contact with the first
> men of his time; he preferred the company of rustic
> ignoramuses. What animated him from end to end of his
> grotesque career was simply ambition — the ambition of
> a common man to get his hand upon the collar of his
> superiors or, failing that, to get his thumb into their eye.
> He was born with a roaring voice, and it had the trick of
> inflaming half-wits. His whole career was devoted to
> rousing those half-wits against their betters, that he
> himself might shine.

I haven't personally known anyone of this ilk, and if I had I
am not sure that I would have been so forthright in what I said
about him shortly after his death. Reading this description
puts one in mind of a certain President of the United States,
though I am less sure of who constituted his betters. At any
rate, Mencken's vitriol was enjoyable.

Mencken was a slayer of hydra-headed idiocy and a mocker
of foolish solemnity. 'A Washington correspondent,' he writes,
'is one with a special talent for failing to see what is before his
eyes. I have beheld a whole host of them sit through a national
convention without once laughing.' Of art critics, he says,
'The more they explain and expound the things they profess
to admire, the more unintelligible it becomes.' Speaking of the

eminent American literary figures of his day who might be deputed to welcome a great writer of another country, he says, 'They all spell correctly, write neatly, and print nothing that is not constructive... To be welcomed by them, jointly or severally, would appear — to Thomas Hardy or Gabriel D'Annunzio as equal to being welcomed by representatives of the St. Joe, Mo. Rotary Club.' Reviewing the biography of the writer of books of self-improvement, Orison Swett Marden, written by the latter's wife, he says, 'His bibliography runs to a hundred or more volumes — a colossal, relentless, overwhelming deluge of bilge.'

> All his books have the same subject: getting on in the world. This was, to him, the only conceivable good of human aspiration. Day in and day out, for three decades, he preached his simple gospel to all mankind, not only in his books, but in his countless pamphlets, in lectures, and in the pages of his magazine, Success. Its success was instantaneous and durable. His first book, Pushing to the Front, rapidly went through a dozen editions.

The strange thing is that the thirst for books of self-improvement goes unassuaged, as if no self-improvement had ever taken place. No matter how many are published, there is always room for one more. In a bookstand in Atlanta airport not that long ago, the books were divided into two classes: Bible studies and self-improvement. Among the titles of the latter were *Fighting Your Battles*, *Rare Leadership in the Workplace*, *Choose to Win*, *The Exceptional Leader*, *The Self-aware Leader*, *The Bulletproof Leader*, and *Leadership Success in 10 Minutes*. Orison

Swett Marden, thou shouldst be living at this hour! America hath need of thee! (By the way, what a name for a writer of books of self-improvement is Orison. An orison is a prayer.)

As for me, I have adapted slightly Polonius's great dictum given to his son departing for Paris:

Neither a leader nor a follower be...[14]

If I had written about Friedrich Dürrenmatt's play, *The Physicists*, a few years ago — say ten or fifteen — I might have said that it had lost its salience, for the risk of nuclear war had receded out of sight, one hoped forever. But *forever* is a word of rare application in politics, and technical progress is often accompanied by a circular movement when it comes to the human wisdom called upon to take advantage of it. As I write this, nuclear war has not seemed more likely since the Cuban missile crisis in 1962.

Dürrenmatt wrote his play at the time of that crisis. As a typical leftist intellectual of that time, he saw little to choose between the United States and the Soviet Union, considering them as mirror images of one another, Tweedledee and Tweedledum. In this, it seems to me, he displayed either a formidable lack of imagination, or a profound hypocrisy. As a Swiss, he lived in a country that, despite its official neutrality, was clearly in the western camp, and he enjoyed all the advantages of living there, including the freedom, without

---

[14] Neither a lender nor a borrower be...

danger, to criticise as he saw fit. The fact that the United States had difficulty in keeping people out, while the Soviet Union had difficulty in keeping people in, should have been enough to tell any minimally sensible person that there was a great difference between the two, whatever the defects of the preferable one.

The action of the play takes place in an expensive private mental hospital in Switzerland. Dürrenmatt's initial stage directions are remarkable in their ironical exactitude: for example, from the windows can be seen the town beyond a lake, with a 'modest university with a recently added theological faculty... in addition... a business school and a Dental School.' He uses the occasion to pass comment on modern urbanism, for it is difficult to see how a dental school could be distinguished as such at a distance from any other banal building in a townscape painted on a theatre backdrop. Of course, a Swiss, Charles Edouard Jeanneret, better known as Le Corbusier, played a central role, through his genius for self-advancement, in making the world safe for ugly banality: though, like all large-scale evil-doers, he needed a zeitgeist and collaborators in his appalling work of destruction.

The hospital is called *Les Cerisiers*, Cherry Trees, not an untypically euphemistic name for a disagreeable or menacing institution (the idea that one can change the nature of a thing by changing its name springs eternal to the human mind). The institution is directed by an aristocratic hunchback spinster doctor, Fräulein Doktor Mathilde von Zoland. She is in apostolic succession, as it were, to Richard III, Quilp and Quasimodo, characters whose physical deformity also denotes, or even causes, their moral deformity. Such a characterisation would probably not be permitted now, and though I am opposed to political correctness and its successor doctrine, I am not sure that this is not a good thing — on the whole. Certainly, I look back on the employment of achondroplastic dwarfs in circuses as intrinsically comic or absurd figures, to raise cheap laughs (though to do myself justice I never laughed at them very heartily or without a feeling of unease), with distaste and even outrage.

The three main characters in the play are the physicists of the title, one who appears to believe that he is Sir Isaac Newton, another that he is Albert Einstein, and a third, called Johann Wilhelm Möbius, who thinks he has discovered the theory of everything, from particle physics to cosmology. This theory could be very dangerous for mankind, insofar as it would give it infinite power to manipulate the forces of nature as it pleases — and destruction always pleases most.

It turns out, however, that none of these three is really mad; they are only pretending to be so. They all want to remain in *Les Cerisiers*, though for different reasons. Möbius, knowing how dangerous his discoveries are, wants to be considered mad so that no one will take them seriously, while the two supposedly deluded physicists have been sent to the asylum to keep watch on Möbius and try to win him over to their respective sides of the Cold War. In this they fail, but not by very much.

Appended to the text of the play are several dicta by Dürrenmatt such as, 'The worst possible turn is not foreseeable, it occurs by accident.' Or 'The more human beings proceed by plan, the more effectively they may be hit by accident.' This is true, or perhaps I should say *true-ish*, for there is surely a valid distinction to be made between what can and cannot be planned, always bearing in mind that what can or must be planned may often, or will always, result in unintended consequences. As Hippocrates said a long time ago, judgment is uncertain.

As if nuclear war were not enough to fear, we now have other reasons to fear the advance of knowledge and technology, particularly artificial intelligence (the natural form being so often lacking). If the use to which knowledge of atomic physics has been put is anything to go by, the uses to which artificial intelligence will be put are far from entirely benign. I leave it to philosophers of mind to discuss the question of whether artificial intelligence is now, or could ever be, real, creative intelligence. I have heard a philosopher whose opinion I respect argue that what appears to be artificial intelligence is just a superior algorithm and does not at all resemble our consciousness or self-awareness. However, we appear to be just at the beginning of the science: it is, perhaps, a foolish man who says, 'Thus far can it go, and no further.' I was, for example, startled to receive from an artificial intelligence platform a critique (for which I had asked) of my own work. Not only did it arrive instantaneously, but it was coherently written (therefore obviously not by a contemporary university student) and made precisely the criticisms that I should have made of my work if I had been asked to do so. My philosopher friend would no doubt have said that this was all the result of an algorithm and was really just a matter of superior collation, but nevertheless I found it… in a word, alarming. Why bother with me, when a machine could write everything I might have written myself?

Of whatever else we may be sure, we may be sure that artificial intelligence, if it does not escape human control altogether, will not be an instrument of democracy but of oligarchy, and not a virtuous oligarchy either. It will not liberate us but bind us in hoops of steel covered with tinsel.

Möbius in the play well captures the malign possibilities of technical progress, without being in any sense a Luddite. He describes his Principle of Universal Discovery in which he unites quantum and gravitational theory:

> I did it out of curiosity... Why play the innocent? We have to face the consequences of our scientific thinking. It was my duty to work out the affects that would be produced by my Unitary Theory of Elementary Particles and by my discoveries in the field of gravitation. The result is — devastating. New and inconceivable forces would be unleashed, making possible a technical advance that would transcend the wildest flights of fancy if my findings were to fall into the hands of mankind.

To which Einstein — the false Einstein — replies, 'And that can scarcely be avoided.' Newton — the false Newton — adds, 'The only question is: who's going to get them first?'

That still seems to be the question.

I met Sir Ronald Harwood only once, at a party whose occasion I cannot remember. He remains in my memory as a smallish man in a well-cut navy-blue suit; I did not realise how distinguished he was, and this was probably as well. The best way to meet famous or distinguished people is not to recognise them as such, for then you can have a normal conversation with them without being either star-struck or obsequious, or without trying to impress them with your own importance. Although I cannot remember what our conversation was about, Harwood, who was certainly modest, struck me as a witty man. At least, he laughed at my jokes.

He came from South Africa, though he had no trace of an accent therefrom, and he studied at the Royal Academy of Dramatic Art. He was an actor who became a playwright, like Granville-Barker (or Shakespeare, for that matter). His most famous play is *The Dresser*, which I find very moving: a reverent but not hagiographical portrait of the actor, Sir Donald Wolfit.

For some reason which I cannot quite fathom, I have the impression of Wolfit, for whom Harwood worked as a dresser for several years, as a roaring and declamatory thespian of a very old-fashioned kind, with a pompous, albeit very clear, elocution. I must be mistaken, for he was revered both by Peter O'Toole and Harold Pinter as well as Harwood[15], and I do not think they would have revered him if he was truly as he appears in my imagination.

The play is not straightforwardly autobiographical, nor is it mere portraiture: it is the working of memory into literary artifact. It is set in the decade before Harwood was Wolfit's dresser, during the war years when Wolfit did indeed tour the country with his Shakespeare repertory company under the shadow of bombs. This was heroic: ill-paid, uncomfortable,

---

[15] Harwood wrote a biography of Wolfit, published in 1971.

easily made to seem pointless in the circumstances. The actors were lodged in cold and cheerless lodgings, the food must have been abominable, the provincial audiences often sparse or uncomprehending; and yet they were doing the work of civilisation.

Harwood's Wolfit, known only in the play as *Sir* (he had not yet been knighted), his leading lady known as *Her Ladyship*, is vain, touchy, self-important, demanding, pompous, ungrateful, overbearing, and yet vulnerable and strangely lovable. For all his faults, he is touched by greatness, and there is an iron probity about him. He is monstrous but inspires loyalty and devotion. I have known great doctors who were of the same ilk: terrifying to their juniors, and yet loved by them, though perhaps in too great retrospect for them to realise it at the time.

Sir wants to write his autobiography but never gets very far: probably, he has not the ability and suspects it himself. He dies after a last, superb performance as Lear on a godforsaken provincial stage, and the Dresser, called Norman, finds the first pages of the projected work, consisting only of acknowledgements. There is, of course, nothing as yet to acknowledge, but he is profoundly hurt to discover that he, who dressed, made up, ran errands for *Sir* for several years, is not among those acknowledged. And yet it is testimony to the depth of his attachment to, even love for, *Sir*, that he should be so upset by this omission, more thoughtless than malicious.

In the last scene, Norman and Madge, Sir's long-standing stage manager who also loved him but also is not mentioned in the acknowledgements, hold the stage in the presence of the recently deceased actor. Norman says to Madge:

He never once took me out for a meal. Never once. Always a back seat, me. Can't even remember him buying me a drink. And just walks out, leaves me, no thought for anyone but himself. What have I been doing here all these years? Why? Yes, well, reason not the need, rotten bugger... Speak well of him? I know what you'd say, ducky. I knew all about you. I've got eyes in my head. We all have our little sorrows.

Madge leaves the scene, but Norman doesn't notice:

I'd know what you'd say, stiff upper, faithful, loyal. Loving. Well, I have only one thing to say about him and I wouldn't say it in front of you — or Her Ladyship. Lips tight shut. I wouldn't give you the pleasure. Or him. Specially not him. If I said what I have to say, he'd find a way to take it out on me. No man will ever know. We all have our little sorrows, ducky, you're not the only one. The littler you are, the larger the sorrow. You think *you* loved him. What about me?

Grief that lies too deep for words is here expressed with paradoxical power: and no man who inspired such love could be inconsiderable.

I cannot but wonder, however, whether future generations, raised on hyperbole rather than on understatement, will understand the depth of Madge's and Norman's feelings. Why, they will ask, don't Norman and Madge weep and wail in the approved psychotherapeutic fashion, and place teddy bears and gladioli wrapped in cellophane next to the body?

What is the point of having an emotion if you do not display it to others? Can there *be* any emotion without such display? What would be its point?

In the play, Sir is older than Wolfit would have been (he was 37-43 during the war years, in his prime, while Sir is old and ill). Sir and Her Ladyship are so called because Sir wants desperately to be knighted and is upset when a fellow-actor is knighted but not he:

> Why they knighted that dwarf Arthur Palgrove I shall never know. 'Rise, Sir Arthur,' said the King. 'But Sire, I wasn't kneeling.'

The Dresser was first performed in Manchester in early 1980. Nothing seems to me very long ago that is within my living memory as an adult, but even within that short time, as it is to me, much has changed. Sir is depicted as being on the edge of cognitive decline or dysfunction. In the dressing room he can't remember which play he is about to act, *Lear* or *Othello*. He thinks it is *Othello* and the stage direction says, 'Sir looks at himself, and then begins to black up.' This would be impossible now.

Norman reminds Sir that it is *Lear* tonight:

> I'd have given anything to see the play tonight. There's you all blacked up and Cordelia saying, 'You begot me, bred me, loved me.' Well, you see, ducky, Lear has been about a bit.

Forty years later, this would have lost its meaning. We have

145

been accustomed, for example, to white Polonius and black Ophelia on the stage (the latter now often wears torn jeans). The directors of modern Shakespeare productions demand of audiences that they both notice the racial difference and not notice it at the same time: that it should applaud the company's 'diversity' but at the same time not see it because Shakespeare is universal and race is of no importance. It is demanded of us that we should be both obsessed by race and indifferent to it at the same time.

Pauline Smith was born in the Little Karoo and Athol Fugard, South Africa's greatest dramatist, in the Great Karoo. Whether this is evidence that the Karoos are, or were, a propitious place, statistically, for writers, I cannot say, or whether it was merely chance. Still, it is curious that two distinguished writers should emerge from a rural backwater in a country not then known for the wealth of its literary tradition. In 1928, the foremost South African poet, Roy Campbell, wrote, in his long satirical poem, *The Wayzgoose*:

> South Africa, known far and wide
> For politics and little else beside…

Fugard's play, *The Road to Mecca*, was first performed in 1984, and is surprisingly apolitical, at least in any direct sense. According to his preface to the printed play, Fugard was inspired by the story of a woman, Helen Martins, who was an inhabitant of the village in the Karoo where Fugard bought a house to escape from the hurly-burly of city life. Martins was regarded as a little mad because she made strange statues which she stood in the garden round her house, and this was not the kind of thing that women did in small South African farming villages. She committed suicide about two years after Fugard bought his house, and after her death he discovered a little more of her history, which he transcribed in the play.

Helen Martins was widowed when she was 50, and only then did she begin to create statues. Furthermore, she transformed the interior of her house by painting and mosaic into some kind of imagined heaven, or at least alternative world. The creation gave meaning to her life, but towards the end she became paranoid and depressed, or depressed and paranoid, and killed herself.

While one could not call Helen Martins' endeavour commonplace, it was far from unique. There is the famous case of *Le Facteur Cheval* (the Postman Cheval) who spent thirty-three years building a fantastic palace known as the *Palais idéal*, the work of an extraordinary compulsion in a man without artistic knowledge or training, that is amazing to behold, truly an heroic effort at creating something perfect — though also mad.

Nor was Cheval himself unique in his effort or determination. From time to time, a perfectly ordinary little house or flat is discovered after its owner's or tenant's death to be decorated with a naïve Sistine Chapel, the obsessional work having taken many years and been the main purpose of the artist's life. One easily resists any temptation to laugh, for here is the creative impulse at its purest, most disinterested — and rarely being without some artistic merit. Even in the small English town in which I live, there is an ordinary terraced

147

house that a recent owner transformed into an extraordinary grotto — not for ambition or bread, as Dylan Thomas put it, but for the lovers, their arms round the grief of ages, who pay no praise or wages, nor heed his craft or art.

The Road to Mecca has only three characters (playwrights these days try to keep their characters to a minimum, for economic reasons). They are Miss Helen, Elsa Barlow and Marius Byleveld. The first is evidently based upon, but not identical with, Helen Martins. Widowed since she was fifty, Miss Helen has become the object of the disdain of the villagers for her sculptural and artistic endeavours, the narrowmindedness of the villagers being the reverse of the coin of their close-knittedness. Miss Helen was married to a good and decent man whom, however, she never loved, but with whom she went through the motions of a conventional marriage. His death therefore did not affect her emotionally, except as a liberation. Her sculpture garden and decoration of her house were an attempt to create a world of her own rather than live in one made entirely by others, a more colourful and fulfilling world than the grey world about her. It is an attempt to reach what she calls her Mecca.

Elsa Barlow is a young social worker from Cape Town, a liberal in the then South African sense, who enjoys the privileges of being the member of an upper caste but knows that the privileges are wrong. She had befriended Miss Helen on a previous visit to the village, immediately taking her artwork seriously and understanding it as a means of liberation from the crushingly narrow existence of her rural community in the Karoo. She, too, has a sadness: she has had a long love affair with a married man who has finally decided to return to the straight and narrow path of marriage and family life with a child.

Finally, there is Marius Byleveld, the dominie or pastor of the local Calvinist church. It would have been all too easy for Fugard to have made him a bigoted, unsympathetic man, or a figure of fun, but he does nothing of the sort. Byleveld is himself a tragic figure. He came to the village just over twenty years before, after the premature death of his beloved wife. He is the only villager still friendly with Miss Helen, who stopped attending church after the death of her husband, a radical step in such a community, and he is secretly and unrequitedly in love with her.

In other words, love has its sorrows for all three characters: Miss Helen, who has lived through a long loveless marriage; Elsa, who loves a man who could never have given himself wholly to her; and Marius who, profoundly lonely, has nursed a hopeless love for many years. No political dispensation will heal the human heart, and tragedy will continue forever, or at least until humanity goes extinct.

Miss Helen is getting on in years, is becoming frail, and her eyesight is failing. She no longer cleans the house, or even herself, properly. The Reverend Byleveld thinks that she ought to admit herself to the Sunshine Home for the Aged, which is very comfortable and where all her needs will be attended to. Elsa, however, thinks that she should not, that she should struggle on at home, even in discomfort.

At one point in the play there is talk of certification of Miss Helen. It put me in mind of the patient I certified in South Africa nearer fifty years ago than forty. She was brought by the police to the doctor's office in the small town in which I was working. She had been found wandering the streets stark naked. The police put her in rear of their *bakkie*, or pickup truck with a cage, and the two policemen had a scholastic discussion outside the office as to whether she should be brought into the front entrance because she was white, or the black entrance because she was mad. It was for them a question of balancing the alarm of the waiting white patients against the loss of racial prestige by letting black patients observe a naked, mad white woman. I cut the Gordian knot by ordering her to be taken into the white entrance, where certification did not take long. What became of her — except that she was taken away to a lunatic asylum — I do not know.

Miss Helen calls her better, imagined world Mecca, a place of pilgrimage. When, at the end of the play, Elsa points out to Miss Helen that she has never sculpted an angel, Miss Helen replies:

> The village doesn't need more of those. The cemetery is full of them… all wings and halos but no glitter… But if I made one, it wouldn't be pointing up to heaven like the rest.

Elas asks 'What would it be doing?' Miss Helen replies:

> Come on Elsa, you know? I'd have it pointing to the East. Where else? I'd misdirect all the good Christian souls round here and put them on the road to Mecca.

I suspect that western audiences might not much appreciate, or care for, that line now. But how easily it tripped off the tongue only forty years ago!

Not many writers, I suspect, have been sentenced to death, held in the condemned cell, and lived to tell the tale. Dostoyevsky and Arthur Koestler come to mind, and also the South African writer, Herman Charles Bosman. Of the three, only Bosman had committed an actual crime: he shot his brother-in-law to death during a quarrel. Fortunately for South African literature, his sentence was commuted to ten years' imprisonment on account of his youth (he was twenty-one at the time). He served only half of his sentence before release.

Bosman is known mostly for his short stories related by the fictional Oom (Uncle) Schalk Lourens. They are about life in the Great Marico in the Transvaal, as it was then called. His characters are, like those of Pauline Smith, the simple Afrikaner farmers in the aftermath of the Boer War. Bosman looks on them with kindly and affectionate irony, but he had no illusions about their prejudices, backwardness, superstition, and sense of grievance. *Apartheid*, it ought to be remembered, started as a form of affirmative action in favour of Afrikaners, who saw people of British stock or culture (which the Jewish immigrants from Lithuania soon adopted) as politically and economically dominant — and oppressive. The *rooineks*, as the Afrikaners called them, the rednecks on account of the redness of the back of their neck exposed to the sun, were the main rivals of the Afrikaners for power, the blacks counting for nothing politically or economically except as hewers of wood and drawers of water. The anglophones reciprocated the disdain by calling the Afrikaners *rock-spiders*.

Bosman died of a heart attack at the age of 46 in 1951. He published only three books during his lifetime, and most of his work was scattered in periodicals that had to be gathered into posthumously-published books. They became best-sellers in a restricted or limited market, but I do not know whether black South Africans ever enjoyed his work. His white characters talk about blacks in a derogatory or offhand way, but this was surely realism rather than endorsement. In fact, Bosman makes gentle (rather than bitter) fun of the Boers' racial pretensions. No doubt bitterness is now the hallmark of strength of feeling, but laughter may run deeper. Bosman was an egalitarian but not an ideological one.

One of his best stories is titled *Unto Dust*. Its narrator is not, for once, Oom Schalk Lourens, but it is told in the first person, though we never discover who the *I* of the story is. The opening sets the ironical tone:

> I have noticed that when a young man or woman dies, people get the feeling that there is something beautiful and touching in the event, and that it is different from the death of an old person.

When a young woman dies:

> She died, they say, young, when she was so full of life and so fair. She was a flower that withered before it bloomed...

That is why:

... there is a good deal of resentment at the funeral, over the crude questions that a couple of men in plain clothes from the landrost's [the magistrate's] office are asking about cattle dip.

Suicide destroys the wistfulness of the death and renders it sordid.

The narrator himself has suffered from an illness from which he was likely to die — malaria, still present in the Transvaal. In his delirium, he imagined the earth as a great graveyard, and later he mentioned this to a friend called Stoffel Oosthuizen, after which they began to philosophise.

There were people who talked in a high-flown way of death as the great leveller, he said, and those high-flown people also declared that everyone was made kin by death. He would like to see these things proved, he said. After all, that was one of the reasons why the Boers trekked away into the Transvaal and the Free State, he said, because the British Government wanted to give the vote to any Cape Coloured person walking about with... big cracks in his feet [from walking barefoot and developing thick plantar skin].

Then Stoffel Oosthuizen recalls an incident from one of what used to be called the Kaffir Wars which now, if Googled, appear under the name of Xhosa Wars. Kaffir, or kafir, was the derogatory (though sometimes faintly affectionate) Afrikaner name for black Africans, which was still in use in the 1970s when I heard the plaintive complaint of an elderly

Afrikaner lady who was lamenting the changes in South Africa in the liberal direction. 'Nowadays,' she said, 'you have to call a kaffir a Bantu, but if you can't call a kaffir a kaffir, who *can* you call a kaffir?'

That suggested to me one of the greatest or most fundamental of human needs, namely that to have someone to look down upon. Is there any group of people in the world that does not look down upon some other, or any individual for that matter?

Like that Afrikaner lady, Stoffel Oosthuizen laments liberal egalitarianism (more preached than practised, it must be admitted):

> The first time he heard that sort of talk about death coming to all of us alike, and making us all equal, Stoffel Oosthuizen's suspicions were aroused. It sounded like out of a speech made by one of those liberal Cape politicians, he explained.

The Cape was always the most liberal of the South African provinces.

In the story that Stoffel tells, he was riding with Hans Welman when they were ambushed by 'kafirs':

> I could do nothing for Hans Welman. Once, when I looked round, I saw a tall kafir bending over him and plunging an assegai into him. Shortly afterwards I saw the kafir stripping the clothes off Hans Welman. A yellow kafir dog was yelping round his black master. Although I was in grave danger myself, with several kafirs making

straight for me on foot through the bush, the fury I felt at the sight of what the tall kafir was doing made me hazard a last shot.

With this shot, he killed him, and then he rode away. Six months after the end of the war, Stoffel and others returned to search for Hans Welman's remains to give him a Christian burial. They found the place all right, but:

> We were now confronted with a queer situation. We found what was left of them. Hans Welman and the kafir consisted of little more than pieces of sun-dried flesh and the dismembered fragments of bleached skeletons. The sun and wild animals and birds of prey had done their work. There was a heap of human bones, with here and there leathery strips of blackened flesh. But we could not tell which was the white man and which was the kafir. To make it all the more confusing, a lot of bones were missing altogether, having been no doubt dragged away by wild animals into their lairs in the bush. Another thing was that Hans Welman and the kafir had been just about the same size…

Then:

> Stoffel Oosthuizen added that no matter what the differences in the colour of their skin had been, it was impossible to say whether the kafir's bones were any less white than Hans Welman's. Nor was it possible to say that the kafir's sun-dried flesh was any blacker than the

white man's. Alive, you couldn't go wrong in distinguishing between a white man and a kafir. Dead, you had great difficulty in telling them apart.

So death was a great leveller after all. Nevertheless, the narrator:

> … realised just how those Boers must have felt about it: about the thought of bringing the remains of a Transvaal burgher home to his widow for Christian burial, and perhaps having a lot of kafir bones mixed up with the burgher…

In his essay on André Malraux, Simon Leys begins his dissent from the chorus of praise by which Malraux's work has been greeted by telling a little story.

A stranger goes to church in a village, not his own, with a famously eloquent priest. After the service, the congregation is in tears, so eloquent was the priest's sermon — everyone in tears except the stranger. Asked why he was not crying, he replied, 'I am not of this parish.'

When it comes to Nietzsche, I am not of this parish either. Indeed, I am not of this diocese, archdiocese, or religion. To changer the metaphor a little, when it comes to Nietzsche, I am like the tone-deaf man trying to be moved by music, or like a Scottish politician trying to understand what people are doing when they laugh.

I grant him brilliantly gifted, erudite and capable of shafts of insight into human psychology, but his admirers, some of whom I greatly respect, generally go much further and also worship him. They think (with him) that he is the greatest philosopher of all time, as well as an incomparable stylist. But I can hardly think of him as a philosopher at all, and as a stylist I find him bombastic, aggressive and unpleasant. I find his scorn of practically everyone, and his self-aggrandisement, pathetic. Freud said that Nietzsche had more self-understanding than any man before him, or probably any man to come. This strikes me as particularly untrue. One possible interpretation of Nietzsche, apart from the fact that much of his life was a textbook case of descent into General Paralysis of the Insane (GPI), that is to say tertiary syphilis, is that he was a timid little bookworm, terrified of women, transferring heroism from the imagined world of conduct to that of the printed page.

I concede the fact that however much I try to read him, I do not appreciate him might be a deficiency in me rather than in him. All the same, I cannot help wondering whether his bullying and hectoring style intimidates people into liking him or claiming to do so. The same might be said of the literary style of Le Corbusier, the Franco-Swiss fascist, whose hectoring accused those who did not agree with him of not *understanding*, of not being able to *see*. This seems to be a successful technique for those who want to make a mark on the world. Corbusier was the Nietzsche of architecture.

Nietzsche's self-glorification is preposterous. 'Until me,' he seems to say, 'nothing. After me, everything.' This is typical of the grandiosity often seen (no longer, of course) in cases of GPI.

Why such pretensions are not laughed at, I do not know. If I were to write that no good book were to be written until this one, I would (rightly) be regarded as off my head. I may be missing Nietzsche's irony, but if so, his irony is to wit what suet pudding is to a soufflé.

I know someone who finds Nietzsche's intellectual autobiography, *Ecce Homo*, deeply moving, and he is a man whose judgment I respect. To me, however, *Ecce Homo*, appears ranting, at best a whistling in the wind:

> It is my fate to be the first *decent* human being: that I know myself to stand in opposition to the mendaciousness of millennia — I was the first to *discover* the truth by being the first to experience history as lies — smelling them out — My genius is in my nostrils.

I am handicapped by not being able to read Nietzsche in German, of which he is said (and says himself) to be an incomparable master, just as I am handicapped in reading the Koran by knowing no Arabic. But by now Nietzsche has surely been translated into English as well as possible, and the above passage is not only immodest, to put it mildly, but absurd. How could anyone ever have taken it seriously?

Am I tearing it out of context? It is not always easy in Nietzsche to say what the context is: he is not, after all, a systematic thinker. I repeat: the grandiosity of what is said here, particularly in comparison with the mundane circumstances in which it is said, is redolent of the grandiosity described by neurologists in the days when syphilis often ended in GPI — followed by the profound amentia into which

Nietzsche descended after completing *Ecce Homo*.

Nietzsche's extolling of pitilessness — the corollary, after all, of his denunciation of pity as an emotion of the weak and resentful — is again a manifestation of his lack, *pace* Freud, of self-knowledge. It is, rather, what Freud would have called *reaction formation* against his own character, which was that of a man fighting against his own sentimentality. There was, after all, the famous incident in Turin in which he was so moved by the plight of a starved, flogged and overworked horse that collapsed in the street that he hugged it on the ground. This redounds to Nietzsche's credit, but it is hardly consonant with his philosophy of pitilessness. The cynic is the mirror-image of the sentimentalist which Nietzsche feared to be.

In his attack on Christian ethics, Nietzsche had a point — up to a point. At the very end of *Ecce Homo* (and therefore one of the last things he wrote), he says:

> In the concept of the 'selfless' and the 'self-denier', the distinctive sign of decadence, feeling attracted to what is harmful, being unable any longer to find what profits one, self-destruction is turned into a sign of value itself, into 'duty' and 'holiness', into what is 'divine' in man. Finally — this is what is most terrible of all — the concept of the *good* man signifies that one sides with all that is weak, sick, failure, suffering of itself — all that ought to perish...

Now there is clearly an element of truth in this: the modern cult of the victim has become so strong that even the most fortunate person claims to be a victim for fear of being left behind in the vulnerability stakes, or of being unable to empathise with suffering. But Nietzsche's is a typical case of taking the part for the whole, or of imagining a slippery slope that cannot but be slipped down. It is surely true that pity can descend into condescension or even contempt, depriving other people of a sense of their own agency, the better for the person who pities to pose as their saviour, thus serving the will to power. It is true also that those who derive tangible benefits from the expression of pity by others may be tempted to exaggerate their weakness and suffering fraudulently to increase those benefits. What starts as a tactic may become a habit, and the habit may become character. But never to feel pity or compassion? Never to show it? Judgment must be shown in pity as in everything else, and where judgment must be exercised rather than adherence to a hard and fast rule, there is the possibility, the certainty sometimes, of misjudgment. But to avoid that possibility is cowardly, and in this respect Nietzsche was a coward. He did not trust his own judgment, and therefore, despite his rodomontade, preferred to exercise none.

When I worked as a doctor in prison, I loved the prison argot. It was often creative, and Dickens would have loved it. 'You're not going to nut me off, are you, doctor?', asked prisoners who were fearful that I might send them to psychiatric hospital, where they thought, correctly in my view, that they were likely to be treated worse than in prison. Another prisoner, accused of murder and returning to prison after his trial, said that the judge 'Lifed me off,' meaning that he gave him a life sentence.

He made it sound as if the judge had merely brushed him away like a fly on his nose to get rid of a mere inconvenience. A life sentence in England is not a sentence that someone shall spend the rest of his life in prison, for what used to be called *the rest of his natural life*, but it *is* a life sentence in the sense that the person upon whom it has been passed is subject to recall to prison for the rest of his life if he should be observed behaving in such a way that he might repeat his crime: for example, if he killed while drinking excessively in a pub and is seen to be drinking excessively in a pub again. This sounds a little arbitrary to me, and the lifers, as they were known, who were recalled to prison were often aggrieved thereby, whether or not the recall was justified.

Since my retirement, I have had no further contact with prison argot. My social life, such as it is when I leave my study, is almost entirely with people of my own type, whom I therefore assume to be typical of the population as a whole. New words come into fashion, and I am surprised when I hear them first. My initial incomprehension reminds me that I am now on the fast track to obsolescence.

One expression whose meaning I did not at first grasp was *gaslighting*: as when a person felt that he or she had been *gaslighted*. What did this mean? Once I learned that *to gaslight* meant to manipulate another person into believing that he or she was unreliable in his or her memory or perceptions, I realised that it must derive from the play *Gaslight* by Patrick Hamilton, first performed in 1938, which was subtitled *A Victorian Thriller in Three Acts*.

Although the play is sometimes revived, I do not think it is very good: it does not have much dramatic tension. The villain gets his come-uppance all right, but there is no twist in the plot, and the denouement is too obvious early on. What virtue the play has is in its atmosphere and its characterisation of the two principal characters, Mr and Mrs Manningham.

Manningham, whose real name is Sidney Charles Power, lives with his wife in one of those mass-produced Victorian lower middle-class houses in London that would now cost more than a million pounds each. He has returned to this house because, thirty years earlier, he killed a rich widow who lived there while he was trying to steal her jewels. He fled the scene before he could find them, knowing them to be hidden somewhere in the house. He wants still to find them and rents the house with his bigamously married wife Bella, whom he tries to drive mad by causing her to doubt her own memory, for example as to where she has placed something — he having found it and placed it somewhere else to cause her to doubt.

The title of the play derives from the gaslight that lit Victorian homes. Manningham, who pretends to go out to his club in the evenings, is actually searching for the jewels in the uppermost floor of the house. When he lights the gas on that floor, the pressure of gas declines in the lower floors, and the lights flicker there. When he returns from the uppermost floor, the lights lower in the house burn brighter.

The Manningham's marriage is cleverly delineated. Manningham is manipulative and domineering. He makes Bella think that everything wrong is her fault. This is a common technique that I heard about from a hundred, if not from hundreds of, patients. It often surprised me that it was so often successful, at least for quite a long time. Why on earth did the victim not see what the victimiser was doing? To an outsider (as to the audience of *Gaslight*) it was all too obvious.

How many women have told me that they feel sorry for the man who beats them, believing him to be the victim of some kind of neurological condition that is akin to epilepsy. 'His eyes go,' they said, 'and he doesn't know any more what he's doing.'

The 'fit' is brought on, allegedly, by something that she, also allegedly, has done wrong, though she often cannot find out exactly what it is. She devotes hours of her mental life to trying to puzzle it out, and this supreme effort prevents her from seeing the obvious. The policeman test comes as a revelation to her, exposing the absurdity of her self-deception. The test involves asking her whether her violent lover would do what he does in front of a policeman. The revelation precedes her reply: of course he would not, in which case he can help what he does. Whether the revelation in itself is sufficient to change her behaviour is another question, but at least she can no longer pretend to herself that the man is suffering from a medical condition. In the play, however, the opening of Bella's eyes to Manningham's criminality comes as a liberation.

One very realistic touch in Hamilton's play (he was primarily a novelist) is that he makes the bully Manningham[16] offer Bella a treat, his sudden generosity and kindness contrasting dramatically with his usual conduct. This is very much what the violent men did about whom I heard from

---

[16] I was tempted to suppose that Hamilton gave Manningham his name in 'honour' of Sir Reginald Manningham-Buller, lawyer and Lord Chancellor known as Reginald Bullying-Manner. But in 1938, he was merely a barrister, probably unknown to Hamilton.

their victims. First, it demonstrated that they were at heart good and decent men; and second, as a corollary, that their rages must have been justified.

No self-deception was too gross to be possible. I had a patient who had been led to a miserable existence by her husband of many years. He made an odd claim for himself: that he was mentally defective, not a claim that, even in days when every kind of undesirable or undesired conduct has been turned into a mental illness, many make. As a consequence of his supposed mental defect, he was unable to do anything such as understand household bills, or anything that required the ability to read or calculate numbers. He was even unable to dial the telephone for himself. I concluded from this that he must be unemployed. Not a bit of it: he had a highly responsible job with twenty people working under his direction.

'Do you really think,' I asked his wife when I learned this, 'that he could do such a job if he can't read or write?'

She replied, both amazed and amazingly, that she had never thought of this before, and I think that she was telling the truth. She said that thenceforth she would change her whole way of behaving towards him. She would no longer permit such absurdities as his inability to use the telephone by himself. She had come into my room crying and left it laughing.

The characterisation of the Manninghams in *Gaslight* is therefore all the more credible, and far from being merely Victorian.

An Egyptian friend gave me a book of Yusuf Idris's short stories, published (and nicely published, too) by the American University in Cairo Press. I confess that I had not previously heard of Yusuf Idris, though he had been nominated more than once for the Nobel Prize. Apparently, he was much put out that the first Egyptian writer to win the prize was Naguib Mahfouz rather than he; I was predisposed in his favour, however, by learning that he was a doctor as well as writer.

Idris (1927-1991) was very good at short stories. He was, so I read in the introduction, a pioneer of the use of colloquial Arabic for literary purposes. The photograph on the dust jacket shows him to have been distinguished-looking, in a well-tailored light-coloured suit, of the kind that only the Egyptian elite could have afforded — or probably have wanted to wear, though nowadays studied shabbiness might be regarded as more chic. One would be mistaken, however, if one concluded from his appearance that he wrote mainly about the Egyptian upper classes. On the contrary, he wrote about the lives of the poor and in such a way that he made them real to us. Lives of such desperation have rarely been better depicted.

There is no sentimentality here. Idris does not pretend that the poor are, *ipso facto*, good; rather, their struggle for existence renders them narrow, ruthless, hard and unfeeling. As for those better off, they appear as exploiters who do not make the effort of the imagination to understand the poor, but judge them by their own, often hypocritical, standards. No solution is offered, no facile political or economic policy that will spirit the suffering away. Religion plays little part in the lives of the people he describes; they are certainly no fanatics. Their religion is customary, a series of inherited rituals and a concatenation of superstitions, rather than a matter of deep or considered belief. They do not question their religion, but it does not provide them with much spiritual comfort or moral sustenance either.

A few pages of Idris can suggest a great deal. *The Funeral Ceremony*, first published in English in 1978, is only four pages long. It concerns a man called Abou'l Metwale, an undertaker, who specialises in burying dead infants brought to the mosque by the parents so that Shaykh Mohammad can pronounce the proper prayers over them before burial. Abou'l is an albino, which could explain his resort to a less than attractive metier. Albinos are regarded in many societies with superstitious horror, and it is no coincidence that he is constrained to earn his life in this horrible way.

> Abou'l stood in the doorway of the mosque while the midday sun poured down on him; snow-white… his bald eyelids, which he tightened against the sunlight, grew redder still.

He brings a bundle containing a dead baby to the Shaykh and tells him to read the prayers. The mosque is not a place of quiet reflection or spiritual refreshment:

> [Abou'l] planted himself more firmly in his place until the Shaykh started his prayers. Then he let his attention drift to the petty brawls that were breaking out all the time between the countless hawkers and their customers standing all round the mosque.

Idris's view of the religion as it was practised could hardly have been more critical. In the mosque there is a half-witted shaykh, 'who wore a red sash and a leather pouch slung over his shoulder,' of which Idris says, 'God only knew what was inside.' Despite being half-witted (surely an iconoclastic way to describe a man of religion in a society such as Egypt's), this shaykh had a motley crowd of people to follow him. 'He was... hitting his beads on an iron tube he was holding, while he kept up a monstrous chant, his voice being even more repulsive than his face.' Idris is a rationalist in a society of the credulous.

A liquorice-juice seller arrives, clashing his cymbals, and Abou'l, by now very thirsty, can't resist buying a glass. 'Feeling his soul revived', he buys another glass: his soul is revived by the liquorice-juice, not by the prayers that Shaykh Muhammad is reciting.

As the Shaykh ends his prayers with two prostrations, Abou'l is suspicious. 'Shaykh, would you swear on your Muslim faith that the boy was properly turned toward Mecca?' For him, procedure is what counts, just as for a modern bureaucrat. 'What is the matter, brother?' asked the Shaykh. 'Don't you trust me?'

The Egypt that Idris describes is a country very low in trust. Everyone is on the make; everyone is trying to cheat someone.

The end of the story is an argument about how many children Abou'l has brought to the Shaykh that day for burial prayers (like Christian clergymen, the Shaykh is paid on a piecework basis). The Shaykh says it is eight, Abou'l says it is seven. They haggle; Abou'l says that if it were not seven, he would repudiate his wife. The Shaykh finally leaves the payment to his conscience.

Abou'l has already paid the Shaykh ten piastres. At two piastres a child, he owes him four more. The Shaykh then talks. Moreover, business is slack; there are too few funeral ceremonies. Abou'l says, 'You should be thankful. Summer's coming, and the epidemic won't be far behind, and you'll be so busy that you won't know whether you're coming or going.'

Abou'l offers the Shaykh five piastres, and the Shaykh, after hesitating, takes it. 'All right,' he says, 'I'll have one piastre more.'

This is an economical but devastating story, combining the appalling death rate of infants with the callousness of the main characters, the shallowness of religious observance reduced to a few rituals and payment of fees, and the graspingness induced by generalised poverty. This is a society of constant suffering, almost unrelievedly so.

Why do we want to read about it? Is it merely voyeuristic to do so? I do not think so, though I am hard put to find a utilitarian answer. Am I a better person for having read it? The first time I went to Egypt, more than forty years ago, I walked in the City of the Dead, the vast Cairene cemetery which it was said that half a million of the living also inhabited. The numbers might have been exaggerated, but the poverty was not. I was deeply moved by the hospitality of these people towards me, who invited me to take tea with them. I felt completely safe among them — poverty is not crime. Perhaps if I had read Idris, I should have felt less safe, been warier, less casually impressed. But would I have been the better person for it?

If Idris's story had been written in 1975, the infant mortality rate in Egypt was 165 per thousand live births. In 2020, it was

15. Poor Shaykh Mohammad!

I have little doubt, though, that there would be other causes or manifestations of human misery that he could batten on to from which to derive an income. There always are.

Often, I wonder what I am going to do when I grow up, before recalling that I have done all the growing up that I am ever going to do. There are actually quite a few things that I would like to do: entomology, for example, or vulcanology, or even antiquarian bookselling. I should like to have been a scholar, a real expert on something to whom everyone turns on the rare occasions when he needs advice on that subject. I should like to have been a scholar of the Dreyfus Affair, of which Charles Péguy said that the more the affair is over, the clearer it is that it will never be over.

It would even be possible to be not a scholar of the affair, but a scholar of the literature of the affair, now so extensive that it could easily occupy a lifetime to read it. Reinach's history of it, after all, ran to 4000 pages and Clemenceau wrote 3000 pages on it. And that is only the very beginning. There is a 600-page book contesting Reinach's first two volumes, published contemporaneously; of the subsequent books, there is a *de facto* infinity. Of the making of books on the Dreyfus Affair, there is no end.

A comparatively short book I read recently on it was *L'Affaire Dreyfus: Verités et légendés* (The Dreyfus Affair: Truths and Legends) by a French professor of literature, Alain Pagès. A specialist in the work of Émile Zola, he is even more specialised in the relations of the writer to the affair. I envy someone who can devote himself to something so narrow, at the same time having added positively his mite to the sum of human knowledge.

Be that as it may, I was alarmed to discover while reading this book that I had quite often written in the vein of one of the intellectual villains of the Dreyfus Affair, Maurice Barrès. He it was who wrote that he was not interested in whether Alfred Dreyfus had actually done what he was accused of having done: he was guilty by virtue of his race alone (Jewish). He was a traitor by nature because Jewish, and therefore loyal to nothing except the interest of the Jews. Therefore, the question of whether he had spied for Germany while a captain in the French army was irrelevant. It was necessary to keep him in prison to defend the army and as a warning to others of his ilk.

We may think this atrocious (as surely it is), but this mode of thought, if thought it can be called, is not only current, but in some circumstances socially all but compulsory. For example, a best-selling book by the American, Robin DiAngelo, titled *White Fragility*, is wholly Barrèsian in its tenor, for it suggests that no white person can escape the guilt of his race. Indeed, if he alleges his own innocence because he has always behaved correctly, decently, in kindly fashion, etc., and even if to all outward appearances this is so, his very allegation just goes to show how deep-seated is his guilt, perhaps even worse than that of a member of the Ku Klux Klan, who at least knows what he hates and does not pretend benevolence. Like the Jews for Barrès, whites for DiAngelo are guilty *ex officio*, the main difference between the two being that Barrès was not himself Jewish.

The book by Professor Pagès quotes a passage from Barrès that I might have written myself. Barrès contrasts the ordinary person who is non-intellectual but possessed of common-sense and normal moral sensitivity with the sickly intellectual, of whom he says:

> Nothing is worse than these bands of semi-intellectuals. [A semi-intellectual is an intellectual with whom one strongly disagrees.] A semi-culture destroys instinct without substituting a conscience. All these aristocrats of thought pride themselves on not thinking like the vile multitude. One sees it too clearly. They feel themselves spontaneously in agreement with their natural group, and they do not rise to the clearsightedness which would restore them to considered agreement with the majority. Poor fools, who would be ashamed of thinking like simple Frenchmen.

I, too, have written that intellectuals, or at any rate the intelligentsia as a whole, are inclined to adopt strange, absurd or counter-intuitive ideas not because they are right but from a collective desire to distinguish themselves from the mass of mankind. This is particularly the case today (I have written) when genuinely good causes on a large scale are difficult to come by, evidence being so complex and ambiguous. Thus the intelligentsia makes great causes out of matters of marginal importance except to a few. Perhaps by the time this is published, the furore over transsexualism will have died down, probably more from boredom than because any truth, factual or moral, has been found and accepted. But the semi-intellectuals of Barrès's disdain will have no difficulty in finding another cause by means of which to distinguish themselves from the *hoi-polloi*. I have thought of holding a sweepstake on what this cause will be, with tickets for such causes as the legalisation of incest (after all, the arguments against it from the birth defect point of view is vitiated by the availability of contraception, pre-natal screening and abortion), necrophilia and paedophilia. The decriminalisation of bestiality in Spain, on condition that the animal does not need veterinary attention afterwards, points the way forward, a beacon to all progressive humanity.

The fact that there is so clear a parallel between what I have on occasion written and what Barrès wrote gives me pause. Barrès is regarded as a despicable figure these days, despite the fact that he was a talented writer (talent in the service of evil is far worse than stupidity in its service). Barrès chose the wrong cause for his caustic pen, and then allied himself to, or became a guide for, people of the worst type.

Does that mean that an argument similar to his in form must likewise be wrong? No historical analogies are exact (which is why they are analogies rather than repetitions). If analogies with the past are to frighten us, we should be reduced to complete inertia. It is possible therefore that the semi-intellectuals whom Barrès despised have sometimes been in the right and sometimes in the wrong when they think and act in a herd. We have no option, then, but to judge each case on its merits: in other words, to become to some degree intellectuals ourselves. There is a limit to how anti-intellectual an intellectual can be.

Is it possible to disbelieve in the existence of God and yet regret the decline of religion? I think it is. This is odd, however. Normally we have a high regard for truth, and if I think there is no God, how can I want more people to believe in Him? (I capitalise the name *God* from respect for tradition, not from belief in His existence.) Do I want people to believe in error or illusion? Is adherence to truth so strong a desideratum that none other weighs in the balance? Sometimes yes and sometimes no. I think lies can be noble.

The French novelist, Michel Houellebecq, is a man who does not believe but would like to do so and who regrets the passing of belief. His problem is that he cannot intellectually assent to the doctrines of his preferred religion, Catholicism. He thinks life would be better if belief were more general, as if assured thereby of transcendent meaning and purpose. Of course, it is possible to believe in the transcendently evil. Transcendence is not a value in itself.

Houellebecq is a chronicler of meaninglessness. Among other things, a sense of meaninglessness disarms you in the face of fanatics. They believe, but you cannot prove that what they believe is evil or will result in evil. The protagonists of Houellebecq's books are always the same: men who have no economic problems, live in material abundance, are intelligent and educated, but who have no real purpose in life. Even culture is for them a kind of Louis Vuitton luggage of the mind, with no intrinsic importance.

Brett Easton Ellis is the American Houellebecq (or is it the other way round?). Houellebecq and his characters are far more sophisticated, intellectually, in that they are aware of the cause of their inner emptiness, but Brett Easton Ellis is ploughing the same field.

I found a copy of his *Imperial Bedrooms* in a charity shop for less than the cost of a postage stamp, which seemed good value to me. I was attracted not only by the price but by the cover: the name *Brett Easton Ellis* in large sans serif lettering on a translucent dust cover with the silhouette of a large devil — *the Devil* — on the shiny cover below. The title, *Imperial Bedrooms*, was in small print on the dust jacket over where the Devil's eyes should be. It was a clever piece of design. I was reminded that a publisher in a small way of business once told me that a swastika on a cover automatically increased sales by a third, irrespective of the book's contents. I did not know what evidence she had for this, but it sounded plausible to me. The sales premium of the Devil might be slightly less, but there is no doubt about our attraction to evil.

Brett Easton Ellis's protagonist and narrator is the writer of film scripts who appears almost affectless. He does not try to ingratiate himself with us because he does not care enough about other people even to try to do so. He is autistic in this respect, and he moves in a completely autistic world, in which others also have no feelings for anyone else. Without really intending to be, he is a kind of evangelist for feelinglessness: we do not care what happens to him or to anyone else in the book, even if what happens to him is horrible and something by which we should normally be horrified. We don't care, and we don't care that we don't care: we have become like the protagonist.

This is not because of lack of skill on the part of the author: on the contrary. It is always dangerous (dangerous in the sense of running the risk of error) to ascribe intentions to authors, especially when you know little of them. Nevertheless, I think it is Brett Easton Ellis's intention to induct us into the mental world of radical unfeelingness.

No character in the book has any affection for any other, and each uses others as instruments for the furtherance of his or her ambitions. On the fringes of the film world, everyone wants to be a star and is willing to do anything to become one. The protagonist — he can hardly be called the hero — who is called Clay has a sexual relationship with Rain (all relationships in the book, more or less, are sexual), a relationship which is, on her part, an attempt to secure a role in the film whose script Clay has written and is co-producing. He becomes obsessed by her, though there is no real substance to their relationship, other than sexual gratification on one side and career advancement on the other. Clay's is nothing like romantic love at first sight: he is completely without a sense of romance. It is more likely that, as an older man, he is trying to flatter himself by the possession of a beautiful younger woman. He attracts her by dangling the prospect of the role before her, though he knows that she is talentless and will never succeed as an actress. He is Harvey Weinstein without the physical abuse, though occasionally he comes near to it.

Clay's world is utterly ruthless, but it is difficult to see to what end. There is no sense of larger purpose to it; the jostling and jockeying might as well be ends in themselves. Drugging and drinking to excess are taken for granted, and Clay thinks nothing of driving having drunk a bottle of gin (the brand name mentioned, of course, for brands indicate position in society). All the cars are German, with the exception of a Jaguar. A man is what he drives: Clay never so much as gets into his car without reminding us that it is a BMW. Incidentally, it is interesting that this book, published in 2010, makes no mention of electric cars and is therefore a technological aeon ago, suggesting that we are now either in the grip of a mass hysteria, or were very slow indeed to realise the harms done by the internal combustion engine — or both.

The sophistication of the society in which Clay moves is that of disenchantment without previous enchantment, of psychobabble in which people talk incessantly about themselves while revealing nothing, of disabuse as the fundamental moral attitude to the world, of the vacuity of existence. The inhabitants of this society are disillusioned without ever having had any illusions. Unlike the character in Houellebecq, or at least some of them, those of Brett Easton Ellis in this book are aware of no culture other than the one in which they now live. They are as parochial in their way as any Guatemalan peasant. For them, Mexico and a Mexican restaurant are one and the same.

The intrigue of the book is hard to follow and would be impossible to summarise. Suffice it to say that some people end up dead before their time, having been horribly tortured first, over the details of which the author lingers with the same salacity as of that of Houellebecq (who is the more talented writer) describing Richter-scale orgasms.

Is Brett Easton Ellis a chronicler or a satirist, or a little of both? Certainly, I have met people who mistook universal disabuse with the world for mental sophistication, and the only time I was in Beverley Hills I watched women who obviously already possessed all that the most ardent materialist could have desired exiting expensive stores with an expression of terminal boredom, clutching what they did not need and hardly wanted.

As far as I know, I have been libelled only once, and that was in the *Times Literary Supplement*. (I am not important enough to have been libelled more often.) At the request of David Sexton, then literary editor of the *Evening Standard*, I reviewed Giles Foden's novel, *The Last King of Scotland*. I reviewed it very favourably, as did everyone else, but J.C., who wrote a weekly column *N.B.* in the *T.L.S.* chronicling very wittily the various forms of pomposity, idiocy and corruption in the literary world, implied in a very short piece that I had in my review been scratching the back of Mr Foden, since I had written a couple of reviews for him while he was deputy literary editor of the *Guardian* and was in effect touting for more work. This was libellous: I would not have known Mr Foden had I passed him in the street, and I had spoken to him only twice on the telephone, and then only briefly. The allegation was completely untrue and without substance.

I imagined my day in court, claiming that J.C. had irreversibly compromised my reputation as an honest reviewer, etc., but I also knew that if I claimed this I would have been lying, since I had no reputation to lose and if I had, this paragraph would not have made any difference to it. I should have had to be as self-pitying as Prince Harry. Besides, I knew the editor of the *T.L.S.*, and one does not sue one's acquaintances. I took the attitude of a slogan I saw painted on the sides of Nigerian buses: *Let them say*. But Mr Sexton made representations on my behalf by letter to the *T.L.S.*, pointing out that my review had said only what many others had said.

A quarter of a century later, J.C. — James Campbell — published a selection of his columns in a book titled *N.B. — A Walk Through the Times Literary Supplement*. It does not specifically mention the piece he wrote about my review, but to my surprise I read the following on page 140:

> My predecessor [on the *N.B.* column], David Sexton, also complained, more severely, in a telephone call, about a piece in N.B. on the subject of a review that was published in the books pages of his new home, the *Evening Standard*. I thought the comment was fair — the editor, Ferdinand Mount, agreed — and argued… that former colleagues shouldn't expect special protection. Sexton was not to be assuaged, and wrote a letter to the editor…

Perhaps this does not refer to my review, and perhaps Mr Sexton complained more than once, but I doubt it. If I am right, this is the nearest I have ever attained to literary eminence.

I do not tell this story to denigrate or express hatred towards J.C., James Campbell, or to take my revenge. On the contrary: I have rarely read a book with more pleasure than I derived from this selection. I read it lying on the grass in the sun and have not laughed so much in that position or situation since, aged about twenty, I discovered the work of the famously worst poet in the English language, William McGonagall, whose greatest poem was *The Tay Bridge Disaster*, which begins:

Beautiful Railway Bridge of the Silvery Tay!
Alas! I am very sorry to say
That ninety lives have been taken away
On the last Sabbath day of 1879,
Which will be remembered for a very long time...

I still recall the tartan cover of the cheap paperback edition that I had bought (and still possess). I had not heard of him until then, and I spent two hours reading it flat on my back. By the end, I was so weak with laughter that I had difficulty standing, but many years later, I came to see McGonagall not as a comic but as a tragic figure, and I felt deeply for him. The son of illiterate and impoverished Irish immigrants to Scotland, he conceived of literary ambitions — goodness knows how — and surely there was something noble in this. I felt I had been rather a swine, or at least a spoilt brat, for having laughed so much.

I won't live long enough to regret my laughter at J.C.'s book, not that I should ever have to do so in any case. No one has ever punctured literary self-importance or pretension with such sure aim as his (apart from the odd misfire, of course). For example, he exposes to justified ridicule Andrew O'Hagan, who selected a certain book, *The Eitingons*, by Mary-Kay Wilmers, as his book of the year in three publications. 'I always want to cheer when something truly singular comes along. Such a book is *The Eitingons*... a small masterpiece of indirection.' This was in the *New Statesman*.

In the *Guardian*, he wrote, 'My prose book of the year is without doubt *The Eitingons*... A completely riveting story of the author's wide family... Patience, irony and indirection.'

In the *Daily Telegraph*, he wrote, 'It was many years in the making, but *The Eitingons…* was worth the wait. Readers will feel rewarded from the first pages.' J.C. comments:

> Ms Wilmers, who is the editor of the *London Review of Books*, must be thrilled. If she wishes to thank Mr O'Hagan, she won't have far to look. He is a contributing editor of the *London Review of Books*.

This makes my own paltry efforts at back-scratching, if such they had been, look very amateurish indeed.

There are many hilarious passages in *N.B. by J.C.*, which I read at two sittings with intense admiration for my libeller. Between the two sittings I couldn't wait to get back to it. The ridicule of our former Prime Minister, Gordon Brown, is delicious, at least for those who enjoy reputation-puncture as a genre. Mr Brown had written a foreword to a book of essays about Adam Smith, in which he said:

> Coming from Kirkaldy as Adam Smith did, I have come to understand that his Wealth of Nations was underpinned by his Theory of Moral Sentiments.

Of this, J.C. writes:

> [Our reviewer for the *TLS*] pondered this and wondered 'how exactly coming from Kirkaldy enabled the Prime Minister to come to his understanding?'

Unabashed, says J.C., 'Mr Brown delivered the Hugo Young

memorial lecture in which he said, 'Coming from Kirkaldy as Adam Smith did, I have come to understand that his *Wealth of Nations* was underpinned by his *Theory of Moral Sentiments*.' J.C. adds:

> The Prime Minister has now written an introduction to the first British edition of *The Roads to Modernity* by Gertude Himmelfarb, which tackles 'such thinkers as Adam Smith, David Hume and Edmund Burke...' He then writes, Coming from Kirkaldy, as Adam Smith did, I have come to understand that his *Wealth of Nations* was underpinned by his *Theory of Moral Sentiments*.

J.C. adds that 'we have come to understand that those who do not remember their own waffle are condemned to repeat it.'

I should think that even Mr Brown laughed.

Henry Arthur Jones was once a colossus of the British theatre — which at the time (he lived from 1851 to 1927) was perhaps not to be so very colossal. Even in his own day, he was somewhat despised: Oscar Wilde said that there were three rules of dramatic composition, the first being not to write plays like those of Henry Arthur Jones. The second and third rules were the same.

Jones wrote many plays, some of them commercially very successful, but I don't know when any of them was last put on. He was often regarded as a George Bernard Shaw of conservatism, and though I am not sure that this was quite fair, a reputation for conservatism is not much of a recommendation in the theatre world or to the public which now tends the other way. And certainly by the end of his life he sounded rather blimpish, if a letter by him found by me inside a copy of one of his plays is anything to go by. The letter is to John Peale Bishop (1892-1944), an American poet. It was presumably written to Bishop during a visit to London. Dated 12 November, 1927, shortly before his death, and written in an elegant, clear hand, except frustratingly for one important word, it goes:

> Dear Mr Bishop,
>
> I've just been reading your article on 'The Function of Dramatic Criticism.' One of these days, (when I get free from more pressing matters) I'm going to write a paper on "The Terrible evils of Impressionism." I believe that much of the disorder in art and in morals is due to impressionist judgments. The lady who took an impressionist view of the seventh commandment found herself in the divorce court. And a man who took an impressionist view of the eighth commandment found himself in gaol. There are great rules in art and in morals. Unless the critic puts these great rules in the first place of honour and steadies his judgment by them, he will be apt to praise what is freakish and eccentric and "modern" in the worst sense. Hence our present want of a clean aim and movement in our English theatre, our want of understanding of Shakespeare, his unpopularity with the mass of playgoers, with all our other wanderings away from the centre. These confusions are only to be corrected by a reaffirmation of great rules and principles,

not by "impressionism". Of course we need firm independent criticism; of course we need the personal view of the critic. But at the present moment we need chiefly a bold assertion and reliance on the great changeless rules. In my nearly fifty years' experience, I have watched the rise of many heretical schools from the [illegible] symbolic school onwards. They have all perished.

Come and dine with us some early evening and bring Mrs Bishop — and my four volumes of plays. We will talk these things over. I had many thoughts I should like to have spoken out at the Critics' dinner but Baughan[17] said "only 10 minutes."

Sometimes, alas, I hear myself speaking in precisely the tone of Henry Arthur Jones' letter to the young American poet.

But it would be wrong to dismiss Jones as a figure of fun, as if he were of no account at all. He was once compared to Ibsen, even if it was always acknowledged that he was on a lower plane. If his morality is not ours, it is salutary to remember that ours will not be that of a hundred years' time either. We have not reached the final destination of enlightenment and wisdom, as the present condition of the world attests (and always will).

Jones's play, *Michael and His Lost Angel* was not a great success when it was first performed in 1895. It ran for only ten nights and was removed from the stage, not for commercial

---

[17] Edward Algernon Baughan, 1865 - 1938, was a theatre and music critic.

reasons, but because the theatre management thought it offended, or ought to have offended, public sensibility. Jones, conservative as he might have been, was not afraid to offend, and in fact was something of a radical for a time, insofar as he insisted on naturalism in an age which largely eschewed it in favour of crude melodrama. Not that Jones was not melodramatic: but he was not *only* melodramatic.

Michael is the Archangel who battles Satan and casts him out of heaven. In the play, the Reverend Michael Feversham is a morally rigorist, or rigid, clergyman of a rural parish whose great ambition is to restore the local minster to its former glory, and then to serve in it. The play is about the conflict between abstemiousness and sensuality, and while this conflict is not seen as black and white, Jones makes it clear that he thinks that flesh has its claims.

Feversham is scholarly — he translates texts from the Arabic — and has an assistant, Andrew Gibbard, whom he rescued from poverty and trained to scholarship. Gibbard's daughter, Rose, has committed a sin of the flesh, and Feversham, who believes in purity, makes her confess in front of the whole village congregation. He then drives her into an Anglican nunnery to repent for the rest of her life. For a modern audience who do not take the idea of sin very seriously, except in matters of carbon dioxide emission, it requires some effort of the imagination (which many are not prepared to make) to find the situation compelling rather than merely cruel or absurd.

As in *Measure for Measure*, in which the morally rigid Angelo does not comply with the standards he imposes on others, Feversham commits the very sin for which he has expelled

Rose. As Rose initially lied about it, so does he. In the end, his conscience compels him to confess before the village congregation, precisely at the moment of his triumph when the Minster is reconsecrated.

Feversham's downfall is Miss Audrie Lesdon, the daughter of an Australian millionaire (at the time, Australia was probably the richest country *per capita* in the world). She is a society woman, half-worldly but also half-spiritual, or at least with spiritual longings. It is she who pays for the restoration of the Minster; Feversham and she fall in love, and they spend the night together (the very sin that Feversham forced Rose to confess). This is all the worse because Audrie is still married, though she tells Feversham that she has not seen her husband alive for two years, from which he falsely, and all too-willingly, concludes that she is a widow. The fact that he has committed adultery as well as fornication weighs heavily on his mind and makes him feel almost exponentially more guilty.

A modern audience wouldn't find this dramatically compelling because no one would make such a fuss over what is at most a private weakness. But still the question of how far we can reconcile our conduct with our principles (assuming that we have any) is important. And notwithstanding the letter that I have quoted, I think Jones' play is a plea for understanding, moderation and flexibility.

When I was young, I was very interested in cricket. Many are the happy days that I spent at Lord's, the large cricket ground that, for much of the time, was empty of spectators. As I have mentioned, I lost interest in cricket as I grew older, my residual interest evaporating entirely when cricket became as vulgar as everything else.

As I have also said, there was still something hieratic about the game when I was young. Applause was measured, and good play by the side one wanted to lose was applauded almost as generously as that by the side one wanted to win. It all seemed fundamentally sportsmanlike and gentlemanly.

What a different world it was then! A career as a professional cricketer in days gone by seems to me now to have been a melancholy thing (H.G. Wells's father was a professional cricketer until he was badly injured). One of the only cricketing books I have ever read — there is an immense number of them — was about cricketers who committed suicide: but though tragic and often moving, it did not answer the obvious question as to whether cricketers were especially liable to suicide, and if so, why. I know that comedians are more than usually apt to commit suicide: my friend Professor Ferner published a paper about the low life-expectancy and high suicide rate of comedians.

Perhaps my greatest cricketing moment as a young boy was when I ran out to stop a fine shot by P.B.H. May from crossing the boundary, much to the disapprobation of the spectators, who were numerous because it was a match of England against Australia. P.B.H. May was an elegant batsman who died of a brain tumour at what I now consider the early age of sixty-three. I held the ball that he had struck with such effortless power almost as a religious person touches the hem of a saint's garment.

As to my own playing career, its finest moment was, in a sense, as a member of the *Spectator* team against the Coach and

Horses pub team. Its glory owed nothing to my sporting efforts but to the location where the match was played: the Oval in Kennington, one of the most famous and the largest cricketing grounds in England. For the first time in my life, I appreciated what it must be like to perform in front of a vast crowd — not that there was any such crowd present.

The most memorable moment in the match, or the one that I remember, was the collapse of Jeffrey Barnard, the Spectator's famous chronicler of drunkenness, who was acting as umpire. I thought he must be dead, but in fact he was merely dead drunk. The clear fluid that had been brought out to refresh him (it was a hot day) was not water but gin and tonic, probably mostly gin.

Subsequently, I played in the odd village game, my wife watching. As she is French, she had difficulty in grasping the rules, which seemingly must be learned early in life or not at all. Understanding cricket unless you have learned it young is like trying to understand the mystery of the Trinity.

I had a romantic view of cricket as being competitive but civilised, in which players would rather lose than cheat or otherwise behave badly. Imagine, then, my shock when I discovered that village cricket had changed within my lifetime and that now even village cricketers employed the same intimidating tactics as highly-paid professionals! They swear, they insult, they menace their opponents. They cheat by altering the ball and by other ruses. It was rather like discovering that the rural dean of the Church of England were embezzling funds or selling pornography.

My rose-tinted spectacles about cricket were darkened when I bought (for next to nothing) a book titled *Cricket in*

Conflict: The Story of major conflicts that have rocked the game. The authors were Peter Wynne-Thomas and Peter Arnold, the former being (at the time, 1984) secretary of the Association of Cricket Statisticians, to which has now been added 'and Historians'. On its current website, its equity and diversity statement now says that it will no longer use the word *batsman*, replacing it by *batter*, as in the substance that surrounds the fish of fish and chips, and as is sometimes used to describe the action of a man towards his female companion.

While I can still recall very clearly the cricketing heroes of my youth — Fred Trueman, for example, and Brian Statham, both now dead — my knowledge of the history of the game was so limited and perfunctory that a few pages of the book were sufficient to overturn my notion of it as the most genteel of sports. Far from it! In its origins, it was often regarded as a public threat or nuisance, and in particular a threat to religion. The authors quote an account of conflict with religious authorities in Boxgrove, a village in which there was still an active Benedictine priory in 1722. A prosecutor of the time said:

> I present Raphe West, Edward Hartley, Richard Slaughter, William Martin junior together with others in their company whose names I have no notice of for playing cricket in the churchyard on Sunday the 5th May after sufficient warning to the contrary, for three special reasons: first that it is contrary to the 7th article, secondly that they use to breake the church windows with the ball and thirdly that a little childe had like to have her brain beaten out with a cricket batt.

And there was a pamphlet published ten years earlier warning of the spiritual dangers of cricket with a title as follows:

> The Sabbath Breakers: Or, the Young Man's Dreadful Warning Piece. Being a very dismal Account of four Young Men who made a Match to Play at Cricket and as they were at Play, there rode out of the ground, a Man in Black with a Cloven Foot, which put them in great consternation; but as they stood in this Frighted Condition, the Devil flew up in the Air, in a Dark Cloud with Flames of Fire, and in his room he left a very beautiful Woman, and Robert Yates and Richard Moore hastily stepping up to her, being charmed with her Beauty went to kiss her, but in the attempt instantly fell down Dead.

The two others went mad.

In my youth I wasted time watching cricket, and now doth time waste me.

Some years ago, I had a little spat in print with Stephen Pinker, the eminent psychologist at Harvard. I objected to his view that a standard language, English or any other, was simply a form of language with an army or navy, that is to say a language whose speakers had the political and social power to impose it on others as the language they must speak if they wanted to get anywhere. He claimed that all forms of all languages were equal in expressive power. He extolled in particular what he called *Black Vernacular English*, and I objected, *inter alia*, that it was surely no coincidence that his book, *The Language Instinct*, was written in Standard English rather than in BE, and that if it had been written in the latter, it is unlikely that my copy would have been of the twenty-sixth printing. I am not sure that this was a good argument, except rhetorically, for he might have replied that this all went to show how strong and effective had been the policing of the language. Presumably, however, there was for him no such phenomenon as untranslatability.

Pinker is mentioned in J.C.'s amusing book, mentioned above:

> Language mavens… are also known as prescriptionists or purists, according to Steven Pinker in his new book, *The Sense of Style: The thinking person's guide to writing in the 21st Century*, as well as 'language police, *usage-nannies*, grammar Nazis'.

J.C., correctly in my view, asks who these persons are and whether there is a single person alive who believes that modern speakers ought to sound like John Dryden? But this is not quite the same as saying that there should be no common standards whatever.

On Pinker's argument, it occurred to me, there should be no such thing as linguistic jokes, depending as they often do on deviance from a standard language. Most of the glorious utterances in Dickens would cease to be funny if the only criterion of language was the conveyance of meaning. Let us take as an example Mr. Bumble's response to the supposition that a man is in control of his wife:

'If the law supposes that,' said Mr Bumble, squeezing his head emphatically in both hands. 'the law is a ass — a idiot.'

If what Pinker calls 'the language Nazis' — how trivially that appellation now trips off the tongue, thereby contributing to amnesia about what the Nazis really were — had care of Mr Bumble when he was a boy, he would have said 'an ass — an idiot' and the whole utterance would have been much less funny. But if the whole purpose of an utterance is to convey meaning, *à la* Pinker, it wouldn't have been funny either, for it conveys very well Mr Bumble's opinion of the law; indeed, it would be wrong to laugh at what he said. For Pinker, when we laugh at what Mr Bumble says we are cruelly mocking those who do not speak a language with an army and navy. After all, *a idiot* means nothing different from *an idiot* and conveys its meaning just as well.

Mrs Gamp is another example of a character at whose utterances we laugh. Poor Mrs Gamp! She was a nurse before nursing in England was a profession. She is fat, drunken and slovenly. She says of one of her patients, 'He'd make a lovely corpse!' When it comes to laying out a corpse, Mrs Gamp says to Mr Pecksniff, invoking her imaginary friend, Mrs Harris:

'Mrs Harris,' I says, at the very best case as ever I acted in, which it was but a young person, 'Mrs Harris,' I says, 'leave the bottle on the chimley-piece, and don't ask me to take none, but let me put my lips to it when I feel so dispoged....' 'Mrs Gamp,' she says in answer, 'if ever there was a sober creetur to be got at eighteen pence a day for working people and three and six for gentlefolks — night watching,' said Mrs Gamp with emphasis, 'being an extra charge — you are that invallable person.' 'Mrs Harris,' I says to her, don't name the charge, for if I could afford to lay out my fellow creeturs for nothink, I would gladly do it, such is the love I bears 'em. But what I always says to them as had management of matters, Mrs Harris, be they gents or ladies, is, don't ask me whether I won't take none, but leave the bottle on the chimley-piece, and let me puts my lips to it when I feel so dispoged.'

This could all easily be put into standard English, for its meaning is abundantly clear, but what a loss it would be to do so! The preposterous attempt at gentility by Mrs Gamp, the slatternly drunkard, would be lost, as well as implicit information about the hierarchical society in which she lives. To get the full meaning, explicit and implicit, of this passage when translated into standard English would require a great deal of explanation; beside which it would be inaccurate, since the Mrs Gamps of the world, who existed and exist still, do speak as Dickens makes Sairey speak. Dickens listened very carefully both to how people spoke and to what they said.

Not to belabour the point, I will give one more example, that of the great pedagogue, Wackford Squeers. Here is Mr Squeers, headmaster of Dotheboys Hall, teaching children not only how to spell, but a valuable practical lesson:

'We go upon the practical mode of teaching, Nickleby [said Mr Squeers]; the regular education system. C-l-e-an, clean, verb, active, to make bright, to scour. W-i-n-d-e-r, winder, a casement. When the boy knows this out of a book, he goes and does it.'

If one adopts the same attitude to orthography as does Professor Pinker to grammar, there would be nothing funny in the above. And, after all, when someone says winder like Mr Squeers, we know perfectly what he means. Mr Squeers, then, is as good a pedagogue as any other.

How far can one carry this school of pedagogy? One (Marxist) interpretation of it is that it is the means by which the possessing classes do not have to meet challenge to their position from below, their children mastering standard language as a birthright, without it having to be taught: for come what may, mastery of that language will remain a key to or precondition of success in most fields of endeavour.

Once, in Australia, I shared a platform with an educationist — that is to say, someone who did her best to prevent or undermine education. She said that she thought that Aborigines should not be taught to read or write because it was not part of their native culture to read and write.

This is the attitude that British educationists seem to have taken to a large proportion of British children.

When I took the little pile of books that I had selected from the shelves of a second-hand bookshop in Nîmes to the counter for payment, the youngish man whom I supposed to be the owner (and hoped so to, for if he were, it suggested at least the possibility that the shop might remain in business) said, 'Monsieur is a bibliophile,' to which I replied, 'No, a bibliomane.'

These two categories overlap, no doubt, but still are sufficiently distinct to be distinguishable. The bibliophile is excited by books as physical objects, by their beauty, or their rarity, or by some slight variation in their edition or printing. The bibliomane, by contrast, is obsessed by books, usually for their content though, like me, he may acquire them quicker than he can read them. He may well prefer an early to a late edition, or a pleasing to an ugly one, yet he never loses sight altogether of the content and does not buy what he does not intend to read or at least refer to, with however forlorn a hope of doing so. I use the male pronoun advisedly, for both bibliophilia and bibliomania are predominantly male oddities of character. Whether this is the consequence of biology or social conditioning, I leave to the reader to decide.

The first of the books I bought in Nîmes was *Mes plus lointains souvenirs* (My Earliest Memories) by François Mauriac, published in 1929. Mauriac was then 44, but he wrote this little book as if it were about very distant times, which in a sense they were. No doubt it is foolish to seek decisive breaks in history, because the past is always irrecoverable, but while the Mauriac of 1929 seems to me almost a contemporary, the Mauriac of his childhood strikes me as a person of a decisively different epoch, thus tempting me to think that there was a profound civilisational change between his birth and forty-four years later, a change greatly accelerated, but perhaps not entirely caused by, the First World War.

Mauriac was a Catholic from the beginning to the end of his days, but his subject was the nastiness of French Catholic provincial bourgeois life, his depiction of which was to win him the Nobel Prize. The curious thing about the Nobel Prize is that it seems to cast a backward sense of destiny on the life of him who is awarded it, as if it were a kind of magnet that from the first drew everything in his life towards it. That a man should write his childhood memoirs at the age of 44 suggests that he considered himself a man of destiny, and not just a common-or-garden scribbler. And the fact is that Mauriac, unlike some Nobel Prize-winners, is still read.

His earliest memories begin with a plaintive sentence:

> I have never grown used to the misfortune of never having known my father.

This sentence, I think, is beautifully calculated to engage our sympathy for the writer, as is the one that follows:

> I was twenty months old when he died; a few weeks of grace afforded by Providence and I would have remembered him; for I can recall his mother, who survived him by barely a year.

The death of his father, at a time when the thread by which life hung was much more readily cut than it is now, affected him and gave him one small advantage as a child. His father:

> … had gone to his properties between Saint-Symphorien and Jouanhant, the recent inheritance from his uncle Lapeyre. That evening, he returned with a severe headache. If, much later, on the day of an examination I

decided not to go to school, I knew that it would suffice for me to press my hand over my forehead with an expression of pain for my mother to be anxious and keep me at home.

Once or twice in my childhood, I tried tricks like that, and they succeeded. Nowadays, I suspect, they have become an adult phenomenon on a very large scale. If you pay people to be sick, they will be sick; and illness that is feigned at first becomes real if it continues long enough. Men do not do what it is in their interest to do but what they think is in their interest to do. Mauriac continues:

> I do not remember my father, but I remember the time when his traces were still fresh; and when my mother opened the tallboy of his bedroom I saw, on the top shelf, a black bowler hat, 'the hat of poor papa'.

The death of his father having plunged his mother and her five children into relative poverty, they went to live on the third floor of his mother's house.

Though his childhood was poor (but not destitute), it was also experientially rich, though this wealth might have been because of the quality of his powers of recollection of it rather than in the nature of that childhood itself. Perhaps all childhoods are rich, if remembered and described with sufficient attention. Mauriac was brought up devout:

> Our nightshirts were so long that I couldn't scratch my feet. We knew that the Infinite Being required children

to sleep with their hands crossed on their chest. We fell asleep with our arms folded, our palms nailed to our bodies, clutching holy medallions and the scapular of Our Lady of Mount Carmel that we did not take off even in the bath.

In bed, the children clung together out of love:

The breath of my mother sought out each of our faces at night. And then she descended to the lower floors where my grandmother lived. I remember the terrible resonant sound of the door that closed behind her. Sleep was the only refuge against such solitude.

In a few words, Mauriac captures the tragedy of his mother's widowhood. In 1929, only eleven years after the end of the war, this was a tragedy known to a whole generation of women (that, and permanent spinsterhood for lack of men to marry), since so much of the male half of the generation had been wiped out in the war. Often in cemeteries I see mute testimony to this tragedy: women widowed for forty, fifty or sixty years, women who died spinsters not because they did not want to marry but simply because there were not enough men to go round.

Devout as the Mauriac children were, they were still children:

At nine o'clock, my mother got down on her knees and we pressed round her dress. My brothers argued over 'the corner' between the prie-dieu and the bed. He who occupied this privileged place buried his head in the curtains that fell from the canopy [of the bed] and could go to sleep from the first words, 'We kneel before Thee, O my God...' and not wake again till the last supplications, 'in the uncertainty of where I shall be if death does not surprise me this night, I commit my soul to you, O my God, do not judge it in your anger.'

An upbringing rich and poor at the same time, full of what we should now consider unbearably physical discomforts, yet conferring, or at least encouraging, a depth of character that is now (I suspect) rare.

The second of the books that caused the bookseller of Nîmes to suspect that I was a bibliophile was *Lettres de Sidi-Mahmoud écrites pendant son séjour en France en 1825* (Letters of Sidi-Mahmoud Written During His Residence in France in 1825). Sidi-Mahmoud was the envoy of the Bey of Tunis for the coronation of Charles X, the last legitimist King of France to be crowned: but the book is not by him. Rather, it is the work of the journalist René-Théophile Chatelain, who used the device that Montesquieu had used in his *Persian Letters* to comment upon, or satirise, French and European society, morals and culture. (The parallels between Montesquieu's *Persian Letters* and *Gulliver's Travels*, incidentally, are very striking.)

No doubt the device used by Chatelain (who lived from 1790 to 1830) would be frowned upon now as being akin to *blackface*: how could a European have the temerity to put himself in the place or mind of a Maghrebin, above all one who actually existed? Never mind that this represented an effort to see ourselves as others see (or might see) us: now that we are multiculturalist, we must stay within the cultural bounds into which it has pleased God to call us — except in the matter of cuisine, of course, for it is perfectly acceptable to eat Mexican one day, Hungarian the next, and Vietnamese the day after, provided, that each is cooked by a person of that nationality. Unlike the sex into which we are born, cuisine is not transferable, and any attempt to transfer it is cultural appropriation. One can know what it is like to be the other sex, even without having been it; but one cannot imagine what it is like to be a person of another culture.

Chatelain's book, published by Ladvocat, bookseller to His Royal Highness the Duc de Chartres, who was later to be Louis-Philippe, King of the French after the overthrow of Charles X in the Revolution of 1830 (but not King of France, an important distinction), is very amusing, a biting but not nasty satire on the France of his time. For example, he has the Bey's envoy remark on the return of Catholicism to power in France after its *de facto* proscription during the revolutionary period:

> We have learned that religious zeal, so long dormant in this nation, has reawakened with renewed vigour; for a time proscribed and disdained, the Catholic faith has regained its empire; that a religious order that, in other times, sent its emissaries into Asia to convert true believers to the Christian faith, now covers France with its establishments [the author is referring to the Jesuits];

and finally, just as at the time of their greatest power, the priests of Christ have claimed and received the right to deliver those who insult their mysteries to the executioner.

The fictional Sidi-Mahmoud remarks on how the honours done him by one of the most powerful monarchs in Christendom demonstrate how proud he is to have a Moslem monarch of the fourth rank as a faithful friend and then, in a passage that would astonish many readers of Michel Houellebecq's novel, *Soumission* (Submission) by its relevance today, Sidi-Mahmoud describes the banquet that is offered in his honour after his release from the lazaretto of Marseille where he had been put in quarantine:

> Since that time, my days have been marked by an uninterrupted train of homages, entertainments and parties. Hardly had I left the lazaretto than when the principal merchants, united as a body, invited me to a banquet to celebrate my arrival within their walls. Although flattered by their eagerness, I thought I must reply with reserve; from the moment I discovered thoughtfulness in these Christians that I had least expected, it was wise perhaps not to let them forget the distance that separated them from a Moslem. The day fixed for the banquet was one of those that our holy law fixed as a fast. I told them that I could not partake of their banquet, since my religion forbade me to sit down to it before the hour after sunset. It is here, dear Hassan [the fictional recipient of his letters] that you see that the

name of Moslem inspires respect in these Christian sectaries. Far from being put off by my reply, they told me that the banquet would not begin until the time it suited me; and, in effect, the guests did not sit down to the feast until an hour after the sun had gone down over the horizon. I will admit that I was so impressed by this act of submission, I experienced a satisfaction so great at having made the Christians fast according to the law of Mohammed, that I relaxed slightly my accustomed reserve; I wanted to mix in with the joy of the feast and I saw that these Christians felt themselves honoured by the familiarity I permitted them.

This continues with another passage of contemporary relevance:

There was in the welcome I received something that seemed to me difficult to explain. Those who were most eager were zealous Catholics who spent a part of their days in church. As such, they must have detested, and in fact did detest, Mohammed's law; where, then, did this eagerness come from? I believe I perceived only signs of admiration, and would say almost of envy...

If one replaced the term *zealous Catholics* by *far leftists*, this might be written today. And the fictional Sidi-Mahmoud points out the seeming contradiction that the zealous Catholics were less likely than the secularists to support the Christian Greeks in their revolt against Ottoman rule.

One passage made me laugh, though not wholeheartedly

with mirth. Sidi-Mahmoud (the fictional) discovers the wisdom of the Minister of Finance. Having been invited to the office of the *Préfet* of Paris:

> When I arrived on the first floor, I saw… it was full of men working very hard. It seemed that not only did they want to renovate the interior of the old building, but to double it in size. I asked the official who had come to receive me what all these preparations meant. He said it was for the celebrations that would soon take place. 'Your custom, then,' I said to him, 'is to raise a monument each time there is a celebration; I am no longer surprised to see how many monuments here. But this custom must make your celebrations very expensive.'
>
> 'The expense is nothing,' he replied. 'Our minister of finance, who is wisdom in person, has as a principle that the more we spend, the more debts we have, the more we grow rich… and we do all we can to reach the peak of wealth.' (I thought a lot about his words, dear Hassan, and I haven't yet been able to understand their sense.)

Here is modern monetary theory in a nutshell, only as satire: and here also is the whole economic history of several countries in the past few decades.

I think the book would stand being reprinted.

The third book that I bought in the Nîmes bookshop was Marcel Jouhandeau's *De la Grandeur* (Of Greatness), published in 1952. I knew almost nothing of Jouhandeau, except the name, before I read the book, and except also a vague recollection that he had been disreputable during the Occupation. Just how disreputable I did not know. In 1937, not long before, he published a little pamphlet titled *Le Péril juif* (The Jewish Peril) and in 1941 participated with several other eminent writers on a propaganda visit to Germany. Unlike some others, however, he was rehabilitated after the war and even became something of a grand old man of letters, though I don't think that his fame ever spread much beyond France.

Jouhandeau was a fervent if not altogether orthodox Catholic. He was homosexual but had feelings of guilt about his impulses to which, however, he gave in. In *De la grandeur* (and elsewhere) he developed a theology or philosophy according to which a man could remain a saintly person irrespective of his outward behaviour, provided he retained an inner sanctity. In the circumstances, indeed in *all* circumstances, this was a very convenient doctrine.

In the book, Jouhandeau develops a detachment from the outer world. First, however, he tells us how sensitive he has always been to human baseness. It was these words, which I read before I knew anything of the man, that attracted me to the book:

> Since my childhood, a blush rose to my face in the presence of ignominy, of vulgar eagerness, of lack of tact, even though I was neither responsible for, nor capable of, them.

He continued:

Since then, so many grave attacks on, so many inexpungeable crimes against, the human person have been committed under our very eyes, that I feel forever dishonoured by my fellow men, whose nature I share.

At first sight, this might be taken as the confession of a sensitive soul wounded by the wickedness of the world, but in the light of Jouhandeau's biography, it might be taken as the very reverse, as a kind of exculpation of himself: for if the world and everyone in it is so filled with evil, Jouhandeau was at the worst only the equal of others, and not particularly bad. After all, he killed no one.

His philosophy is summarised in the following:

It is good to abstract oneself for a moment from history and from the present, to disembarrass oneself from all the ideas of class, of political regime, of species, that one will soon be obliged to take up again as soon as one puts on clothes, a mask or a livery.

Here is the idea of *the real me* that I heard many times in the prison in which I once worked. Guilty of the most appalling crimes, not denying that they had committed them, the prisoners would often claim that it was not their true selves that had committed them, the evidence for this being that the true, the real, them did not do such things. I remember once overhearing on a radio the mother of a boy who had just been caught committing his two hundred and fiftieth burglary, or thereabouts, saying to the interviewer that 'he's a good boy, really'; in other words, *à la Jouhandeau*, there subsisted in him a much better and more real person than the one who had merely broken into two hundred and fifty houses.

Jouhandeau was a stylist, and like many stylists was apt to take an *aperçu* as the whole of the truth. In fact, he wasn't very attached to the idea of truth:

> Some illusions are so beautiful, so noble, that they are more true than if they were true, as soon as they deserve to be. And so much the worse for truth if it is nothing but ugliness, platitude, mediocrity, nothingness.

Jouhandeau's egotism has an almost mystical, or pseudo-mystical, quality:

> The supreme poverty is not to be happy to the point of intoxication with what one has, with what one is.

This seems to me a dangerous elision of two very different things. To be content with what one has is very different from being content with what one is. The former, within bounds, is part of wisdom; the latter, if taken literally, is an invitation to psychopathy. As a burglar once said to me when I asked him why he continued to burgle, 'I'm a burglar, burglary's what I do.' For him, the question was the same as if I had asked him why he continued to have blue eyes: he was a burglar by essential nature and was perfectly at ease with himself for being such. Jouhandeau would have approved.

'Among men,' he said, 'only he is free who turns away from everyone else, to live the interior life… Nothing further from the soul than the city, than politics.' One might wonder, then, why so noble or ethereal a soul had ever bothered to write an antisemitic pamphlet — or for that matter any other kind of book or pamphlet. All that counts is the cultivation of the inner, which is to say the real, man. He says:

> Without affectation, naturally, I am sure that I have never written the word 'social', which expresses what is furthest from me in the world. 'Social' is at the antipodes of what could interest me.

Such a person, say a hermit in the Syrian desert subsisting on locusts and honey as he cultivated his relationship with God, would not, I surmise, have accepted an invitation to visit Nazi Germany as an honoured guest, least of all in the middle of an occupation. There is, to me, something bogus about Jouhandeau's protestations of spirituality, something of the covering of his tracks. In this he reminds me of Emil Cioran, a writer who has survived better than Jouhandeau. There is in Cioran's elegantly disabused, world-weary aphorisms, nihilistic in their rejection of the possibility of any positive engagement with the everyday world, including that of politics, a similar covering of tracks, for he was as a young man an apologist of fascism in Romania, than whose fascism no fascism was more fascist.

And yet at times Jouhandeau has insights that are at least partly, and sometimes wholly, true. He tells us that the central mystery of human existence is that of how we come to be what and who we are: and surely no one can claim to know it of himself. How does one achieve or come into consciousness? However much we think we can explain this in others, we cannot explain this in ourselves. And yet at the same time we are, or feel we are, responsible for who or what we are. To me, at any rate, this is mysterious — as I hope it always will be.

Jouhandeau, ever the egotist, speaks to God as man to man, or God to God. He says to God, 'I do not ask of you to obey me. It is not a matter of that between two beings who respect each other... I mean, two beings who respect their limits, the contour appropriate to each, their 'respective' limits.' I should have thought believers would find this blasphemous in the extreme; certainly, it is grandiose.

But Jouhandeau does point to a puzzle that has troubled me on my travels, in odd corners of the world such as North Korea:

> In the exercise of my duties as a citizen, a believer, a son, a husband, a father, a teacher, a writer, I am more or less conditioned, but there is a secret region that concerns only me, where no one has the right to look, that I rule as I wish, where I look on everyone else as being so far away that I hardly acknowledge their existence.

It is this inviolable secret place that totalitarian governments seek to destroy. Do they ever entirely succeed? Did they succeed in North Korea? Did Winston Smith *really* love Big Brother?

Out of interest, I read Jouhandeau's pamphlet of 1937, *Le Péril juif*. I discovered to my surprise that the cheapest copy of the original sold on the internet was at 500 euros, due to its rarity in what booksellers delicately call 'commerce'. Who, I wondered, was prepared to pay such a price for so slender a work, thirty-two pages long, with only twenty-seven of text? Bibliophiles, neo-Nazis, or perhaps neo-Nazi bibliophiles? Collectors of arcane political pamphlets (of which I have quite a number)?

I found a facsimile copy for a sum I could afford and was prepared to pay and ordered it in the hope that the bookseller would not rush to conclusions about me. It duly arrived, and on the inside of the back cover it informed me that it had been printed by the *Typografia Dezrobirea Proletara* (Proletarian Liberation Printers) in Ploesti (an oil town in Romania). This suggests a left- rather than a right-wing sensibility, but this should not be altogether surprising. In nineteenth century France, for example, antisemitism was left- rather than right-wing, at least until the Dreyfus Affair. There is a good reason, or explanation of this: if you hold that the capitalist economic dispensation is fundamentally unjust and exploitative, then those who benefit from it disproportionately are themselves unjust and exploitative. Therefore, if Jews — not all of them, but a disproportion of them — are highly successful, it is hardly surprising that they should be reprehended as a group. Marx himself, Jewish by descent, claimed that the pursuit of money was the *raison d'être* of Jews and Judaism.

The facsimile of Jouhandeau's pamphlet was, as far as I am able to tell, an exact one. The seller thought it dated from some time in the 1990s. The fact that it was produced in Romania is not very reassuring, given that Romania was the most antisemitic of European countries before and during the war, the Romanians on the Eastern Front rivalling the

Germans in bestiality. Was the facsimile produced from historical interest only, for commercial reasons, or from ideological sympathy? I suspect the latter but cannot prove it; after all, French was, until recently, the first foreign language spoken, at least by intellectuals, in Romania.

The pamphlet consists of three articles, the last dating from July, 1937. It was published by Fernand Sorlot, and the works advertised on the back cover include *L'Avenir de l'Allemagne* (The Future of Germany) by one Adolf Hitler, and *Les protocôles des Sages de Sion* (The Protocols of the Elders of Zion), whose author is given as *XXX*.

Sorlot was once successfully sued in the French courts by Hitler for having published an unauthorised and unexpurgated version of *Mein Kampf*. In 1934, the year of publication, Hitler did not want the French public to know just how aggressive were his plans or what he really thought of the French. Hitler won his case for breach of copyright, and the whole edition had to be pulped; I assume it became a valuable collector's item.

Sorlot did not publish such literature alone: he published translations of P.G. Wodehouse, for example, and of John Middleton Murry's book on Katherine Mansfield. After the liberation from the occupation, however, he was accused of collaboration, all his property was seized, he was forbidden to resume his business, and he was sentenced to twenty years' loss of civil rights. In practice, though, his disgrace did not last long, and he resumed publishing. He died in 1981.

As I write this in my house in France, the country is in the grip of riots occasioned by the shooting of a 17-year-old boy by the police. This gave Jouhandeau's pamphlet an added frisson, because its premise and conclusion (they are, in fact, one and the same) is that there is an unassimilable racial minority that is undermining or destroying France, precisely what many French people think is the case today, though the minority of which they believe it has changed. The North Africans have replaced the Jews as the object of such fears.

There are, of course, relevant differences between the two cases, which I need hardly emphasise. Recollection of a shameful past, while morally salutary, should not paralyse a country in its self-defence or prevent it from acknowledging a very real problem today. It should rather act in a way that the clown acted at the triumph of a Roman emperor, to remind him that notwithstanding his triumph, he was still a mortal. Jouhandeau's *Le Péril juif* should remind the French (and others) how easy it is to fall prey to conspiracy theories and to passionate hatreds, and to the consequences to which these might lead: but not cause impotence in the face of widespread social disorder.

Jouhandeau begins his pamphlet thus:

> When I left my province, aged nineteen, I did not know what a Jew was. During the thirty years that I have lived in Paris, I have frequented many Jews of all types, and I must admit that I have never found them other than friendly and sympathetic... It is therefore not from personal interest, envy or rancour that I came to consider Jewish people as the worst enemy of my country, the internal enemy.

Referring to a brilliant *Polytechnicien*, a graduate of the most elitist (in the best sense) of French educational establishments, who was indifferent to the Jewish 'threat', Jouhandeau writes:

> What dangerous indifference! Hardly 450,000 Jews resident in our country, that is to say a twenty-fifth of our population [an erroneous statistic], and they are everywhere, we see only them, hear only them. They take possession of everything: politics, finance, commerce, industry, art, literature, and there is no reason to be alarmed?

It is not because they are gifted or hard-working that they are successful but because of 'their monstruous avidity and our natural modesty, their natural insolence and our natural politeness.'

Jouhandeau's characterisation might have come straight out of Nazi propaganda:

> Never creative except by accident, the Jew is born to use the work of others, and his activity being the result of his restlessness, and his activity being the function of his restlessness, his restlessness having no limits, he pursues his ends feverishly, without pause, tirelessly… No more that he bends his back to cultivate the land is he a born painter, musician or writer. But if he becomes one, he beats his drum; he commercialises his work straight away. His genius is for publicity. But what a marvellous speculator on the wheat grown by others! What a clever art dealer! What a virtuoso! What an actor! What a critic! What a publisher! Above all, what a politician! And it is

because politics par excellence is the art of using others! In summary, to characterise the work of the Jew, and to stigmatise him [correctly] at the same time, it suffices to consider him under the aspect of the most imperial of parasites, the louse of poultry, the louse of silk, the louse of wool, the louse of wheat, the louse of France, of England, of Europe, of the whole world.

The Jew, communist and capitalist at the same time, is so dangerous that the reaction against him must be immediate:

If it is delayed, it will be all the more terrible, such that this cry of alarm could be more useful than harmful to the Jews, and if they but realise it and deliver us from their presence.[18]

So the lice should take themselves off — but to where, since they would remain what they were wherever they went?

Jouhandeau did not include this pamphlet in his collected works, for it rather contradicted his insistence on the cultivation of the inner person rather than engagement in the world.

Dorothy Edwards was a Welsh writer of short stories who died even younger than Katherine Mansfield (with whom she has been compared), though eleven years later. Her death was, if

---

[18] Jouhandeau had a particular hatred for Jean Zay, minister of education until 1939. He was murdered by the Milice in 1944.

anything, even more tragic than that of Mansfield: she threw herself in front of a train in Caerphilly in 1934. She had a note in her pocket in which she said that she was killing herself because she had never sincerely loved anyone, though she had been in receipt of love. There is no record, as far as I know, of what the train-driver thought, though most train-drivers are profoundly affected for the rest of their lives by such an event. But I suppose it is not reasonable to expect suicides by this method to think of this in the last extremity of their own misery.

Usually, an early death is very good for a writer's reputation, but for some reason it did no good in Dorothy Edwards' case, perhaps because Caerphilly is not redolent of romantic angst but rather of industry, coal-mining, and a certain kind of cheese. Besides, Welsh writers for some other reason are often not appreciated at their worth, perhaps because so few people are interested in the country, or are even contemptuous of it, without knowing anything about it or anyone who comes from it. I once told the late Professor Norman Stone[19] that I was very fond of Wales, and he said (in his broad Glaswegian accent), 'That is the only error of judgment I've ever heard you make.'

Dorothy Edwards' collection of stories, *Rhapsody*, was published in 1928, when she was only 24, but already it is infused with a deep melancholy or even despair. Men in her stories fall in love with the wrong women: for example, Joseph Laurel in the story *Summer-Time*, who falls in love with Leonora, the cousin of Beatrice. Leonora is hardly more than

---

[19] The distinguished late historian.

a schoolgirl, and it is obvious that Beatrice would be more suited to him, being closer to his age. When Joseph sees Beatrice flirting with a young man called Basil, he feels humiliated by his own silliness, so much so that he decides to leave the country for good. Though the cause might seem slight, the wound is very deep, and the empathy for her character seems at variance with both her age and her lack of empathy, seven years later, for the train driver who ran over her.

There is, in fact, very little Welsh about her stories, and one might have thought that she had been raised in suburban Surrey rather than in Ogmore Vale, a small mining village in Glamorgan. She sets her stories among the middle class of her time, who lived at greater ease than the same stratum today, relieved as they were of the tedium of cleaning, cooking etc., by the employment of domestic servants, then taken for granted; and even if not extremely rich, they are able 'to take houses', that is to say rent them, for the summer. None of them has to worry about where money comes from, and the nearest they come to paid employment is giving music or German lessons. These advantages notwithstanding, their lives are emotionally blighted.

It is true that in the story that gives the book its title, *Rhapsody*, two of the main characters, a man called Everett and a woman called Antonia, find happiness, but only at the expense of someone else's tragedy, namely that of Mrs Everett.

This is not a vulgar murder story, such as I might write. Everett and Antonia do not kill Mrs Everett in order to obtain their happiness: from the outset she is very ill and like to die.

Everett decides to take his wife on holiday to Scotland for

the sake of her health. They have a son called Vincent who will go with them. Everett advertises by a 'carefully-worded' advertisement in the newspaper for a governess for Vincent who can teach him music and other subjects while they are in Scotland. Mrs Everett is an accomplished pianist but cannot play any more because of her illness. The governess chosen is Antonia, who has a beautiful singing voice. Everett's ecstasy over her singing is soon disguised love for her. In Scotland, Mrs Everett's condition — probably tuberculosis, considering the year in which the story was written — deteriorates rapidly. She has seen and observed what is occurring between her husband and Antonia. Now close to death, still in Scotland, Mrs Everett says, opening her eyes for the last time, 'Don't let me be buried here.' She does not want to lie forever where her husband fell in love with another woman.

This, I think, is a very piercing scene. Of course, a rationalist would say, 'What does it matter where she is buried since she will be dead?', but somehow this question seems a shallow response to the tragedy. I should not want to be buried at a location in which my whole previous life had been put in question as was Mrs Everett's, and I don't think rational argument would persuade me otherwise.

My mother told me that my father wooed her while his first wife was dying of cancer. Did she (his first wife) know? I certainly hope not.

My edition of this book — subsidised by the Welsh government — has an undated photograph of Dorothy Edwards as a frontispiece. It is a very striking photograph, or perhaps I should say a photograph of a very striking woman. I would guess that she was about thirty, a woman of the most decided character. She stands with her left hand on her hip, in a dark dress, staring almost defiantly into the camera. She has prominent cheekbones and on her voluptuous mouth there plays or hovers something between a smile and a pout. Her eyes blaze. She holds one of her hands before her, and it is large and muscular. If I had seen it alone, I should have thought it was a man's hand.

I suspect that a woman of such strong character, middle class if not above, would not have had an easy passage in her time and place: or for that matter that she would have given an easy passage to others.

Would I have read all this into her face and bearing had I known nothing of her biography, or had not read any of her stories, in which the only happy ending — after his wife's death and the possibility of union with Antonia, Everett had 'a look of intolerable joy [which] seemed as if it would never go away until he died of the intensity of it' — is bought at the price of an intolerable tragedy?

I think I should have guessed that she was not made for happiness, and perhaps not for goodness either.

Leafing through Lord Byron's long satirical poem, *Don Juan*, my eye alighted on the following stanza in the Eleventh Canto:

> John Keats who was kill'd off by one critique,
>   Just as he promis'd something really great,
> If not intelligible, without Greek
>   Continu'd talk about the gods of late,
> Much as they might have been suppos'd to speak.

Poor fellow! His was an untoward fate;
'Tis strange the mind, this very fiery particle,
Should let itself be snuff'd out by an article.

This struck me as not funny, but rather as authentically nasty and unfeeling, cynical in the worst possible way. Whether it was all the worse for having been written only very shortly after Keats's unhappy and untimely death, I am not sure, though I feel that it was. At any rate, it justifies the words on Keats's tombstone in Rome's Protestant Cemetery: This Grave contains all that was Mortal of a YOUNG ENGLISH POET, who, on his Death Bed, in the Bitterness of his Heart, at the Malicious Power of his Enemies, desired these Words to be engraven on his Tomb Stone: Here lies One whose Name was writ in Water, Feb. 24th 1821.

Keats, of course, died of tuberculosis, like his brother, and I suppose that it is possible that his disappointment at his lack of recognition as a poet hastened his end. After all, state of mind affects the progress of disease, even if it does not cause it alone. Keats was particularly embittered by the reviews John Wilson Croker and J.G. Lockart (Walter Scott's biographer) of his poem *Endymion*. Keats had been an apothecary and Lockhart wrote:

It is a better, and a wiser thing, to be a starved apothecary than a starved poet, so back to the shop, Mr. John, back to the plasters, pills and ointment boxes.

There could hardly have been written anything more wounding to Keats, who preferred to starve as a poet than eat as an apothecary.

At least Wilson and Lockhart wrote while Keats was still alive, treating him as someone to be criticised rather than merely sneered at after death. Byron died three years after Keats (poetic justice?), but no subsequent poet wrote lines such as:

> To Greeks, their hopes to flatter,
> Went Lord Byron, the limping satyr,
> There on a bed feebly to die,
> Very close to Missolonghi.

One might interpret Byron's stanza as revenge on a younger man whom he knew to be greatly his superior as a poet, despite his lack of a classical education, his inferior social status and his unconsummated love affair with Fanny Brawne, unconsummation being a concept unknown to the noble lord. How easy to mock Keats's lack of Greek which, however, gave rise to a poem, *On First Looking into Chapman's Homer*[20]:

> Then felt I like some watcher of the skies
> When a new planet swims into his ken;
> Or like stout Cortez when with eagle eyes
> He star'd at the Pacific — and all his men
> Look'd at each other with a wild surmise –
> Silent, upon a peak in Darien.

Notwithstanding their historical inaccuracy, these lines are

---

[20] Chapman's was a standard translation of Homer.

finer, or at least move me more, than anything Byron ever
wrote.

By strange coincidence, I opened later that day a book of
poems by Christina Rosetti, and it fell open at her sonnet *On
Keats*:

> A garden in a garden: a green spot
>> Where all is green: most fitting slumber-place
>> For the strong man grown weary of a race
> Soon over. Unto him a goodly lot
> Hath fallen in fertile ground; there thorns are not,
>> But his own daisies: silence, full of grace,
>> Surely hath shed a quiet on his face:
> His earth is but sweet leaves that fall and rot.
> What was his record of himself, ere he
>> Went from us? *Here lies one whose name was writ
>> In water*: While the chilly shadows flit
>> On sweet Saint Agnes' Eve; while basil springs,
>> His name, in every humble heart that sings,
> Shall be a fountain of love, verily.

This is far from Christina Rosetti's finest sonnet, but it is
incomparably more generous than Byron's snide lines, and its
feeling is genuine. I do not find *spot* a poetic word for place —
surely *plot* would have been better? As for *rot*, I have a fixed
aversion to the word in poetry, especially as a rhyme. This
aversion derives from an early verse of mine, written when I
was about thirteen, an *Ode to a Dead Duck*, which I saw in the
park (I have never seen one dead of natural causes since):

Poor dead duck, you are forgotten,
Nay and more, you are rotten.

Luckily, the world has been spared further such poetic efforts on my part.

The line 'Shall be a fountain of love, verily' is to me beautiful, even if humble hearts these days do not read Keats.

Byron's verse raises the question of whether there is a proper limit to satire. Surely Keats was not a proper subject of satire; a great poet, a generous man, who suffered much through no fault of his own and who died at a tragically early age. To say that Byron should not have written his heartless and shallow lines is not, of course, to say that they should have been censored. Rather, he should have censored himself. His laughter in this verse is cheap, vulgar and nasty.

On the subject of ungenerous estimates of poets, I happened recently upon a book of Cyril Connolly's essays, *The Condemned Playground*. I daresay Cyril Connolly is scarcely remembered these days, though he was still writing book reviews in the Sunday newspapers when I was a boy. I like reading literary essays, even about an author I have not myself read, even about authors of whom I have never heard. But I also like reading about authors of whom I know something.

Connolly suffered from the fact that he was an ugly little man, very porcine in appearance. I have often thought of writing an essay on the mordant literary style of hunchbacks (most of them victims of Pott's disease of the spine, that is to say tuberculosis of the bone, of which I once treated much, though the disease has now largely disappeared in the western world)[21]; I think ugliness might have a similar effect, giving rise to a dialectic between brittle asperity and self-pity. Certainly, no man ever made such a career of self-proclaimed failure as Cyril Connolly.

Failure is in the eye of the beholder, of course. If you continue to compare yourself with Mozart, you will always be a failure. Connolly famously said that the only proper end of a writer is to produce a masterpiece, which he signally failed to do, but his dictum is obviously false and rather shallow when set beside Dr Johnson's view that literature of the second order or rank had its place and its virtues. One should always strive to write well, even of (say) the weather, without any illusion as to the immortality as literature of what one has written. Even assuming that books could be easily divisible into masterpieces and the rest, which is doubtful to say the least, a bookshop that contained only masterpieces would be small — and boring into the bargain.

Connolly's judgment was always firm but not always sound. For example, a review of a book by Karen Horney, *New Ways in Psycho-Analysis*, written in 1940, begins:

> Psycho-analysis leads to the most profound discoveries man has made about himself.

---

[21] An early memory of mine is of a visit to an orthopaedic hospital in which my closest friend of the time, who was afflicted with paraplegia consequent upon polio, was staying briefly. I remember a young man in a bed who was put out in the sun because exposure to the sun was supposed to beneficial in cases of Pott's disease.

This is sheer nonsense, for it is impossible to enumerate a single such discovery such as Harvey's discovery of the circulation of the blood.[22] Freud did not discover: he asserted. Connolly follows up his categorical statement by saying, truly:

> Yet most people would agree that its results have been disappointing.

Here he shows himself to have swallowed whole and uncritically the argument by which psychoanalysis tried to assure its own immortality: what started as a clinical method to cure certain people became a means of understanding the psyche of everyone, once it became clear that it was useless as a cure of anything, probably less useful than a witch-doctor throwing bones, and certainly more damaging to the personality than witch-doctoring.

But back to Cyril Connolly and A.E. Housman, the poet about whom he wrote ungenerously. He wrote his assessment, which was followed by a flurry of letters, three weeks after Housman's death in 1936. Perhaps no man who puts his work before the public has a right to complain if it is criticised, even unfairly; but I could have wished that Connolly had published his appraisal, which must have been long maturing, before Housman's death, so that the poet might have answered. Perhaps Connolly refrained from respect for age, but it was more likely from cowardice. Housman was a prickly, and witty, customer, who thought of and wrote down barbs for future use in reviews, the only man I have heard of who did

---

[22] Actually, even this has been disputed.

such a thing. He was not easy to get the better of.

We now know a lot more about Housman than Connolly could have done, and I think that an awareness of the poet's life *does* affect (favourably) an appreciation of the emotional depth of his poetry. For Housman was a homosexual who fell in love with a fellow-student at Oxford, Moses Jackson, who was, however, heterosexual. Housman was faithful, Miss Havisham-like, to this impossible love, and even if we find this absurd, there being so many fish in the sea, it is still tragic. Connolly could have known none of this: in 1937, for example, Laurence Housman, in his memoir of his brother, wrote:

> … he was provokingly reticent, finding, I think, a certain pleasure in baffling injudicious curiosity. Out of that reserve the journalistic mind has endeavoured to construct a hidden romance which was non-existent, and to suggest some 'lost lady of old years' was the cause of the secluded and celibate life which he adopted in early manhood, and persisted to the end… he chose the habit of life which best suited him.

Far be it from me to extol the journalistic mind, which I share, but in this instance the journalistic mind was right, and the brother was wrong — or untruthful.

Anyhow, Connolly's charge against Housman is that his emotions are commonplace in an adolescent way (his contemporary, George Orwell said much the same thing), and the melancholy expressed immature and shallow. Moreover, his versification was likewise commonplace and clumsy, his images trite: he presents no difficulty, such as T.S. Eliot does, difficulty being here a term of praise. Housman, in his lecture, *The Name and Nature of Poetry*, implicitly answered this criticism, by saying that it was not the function of poetry to express original thought, and that for him poetry had to have primarily a strong emotional impact. This might have seemed strange from a man as outwardly unemotional as he.

An emotional impact Housman's poetry has certainly had on millions of people, but for litterateurs this is not a compelling argument. To quote Noel Coward, 'Strange how potent cheap music is.' This is beside the point in Housman's case, though. Connolly quotes the lines:

> Clay lies still, while blood's a rover;
> Breath's a ware that will not keep...

This, says Connolly, is both tritely expressed and banal of thought, but I do not think so: not unless Ronsard's '*Cueillez dès aujourd'hui les roses de la vie*' or Shakespeare's 'What's to come is never sure' is tritely expressed and banal of thought. Was Gray being similarly true and banal when he wrote:

> The boast of heraldry, the pomp of power,
>   All that beauty, all that wealth ever gave,
> Awaits alike th'inevitable hour:
>   The paths of glory lead but to the grave...?

Is 'Vanity of vanities, all is vanity' a trite and banal statement? Is there, could or should there be, an end to mankind's descant on its own mortality, of which nothing new can be said?

Connolly objected to the incantatory words that follow the lies he quoted, but he does not quote them in full:

> Up, lad, when the journey's over
> There'll be time enough to sleep.

This is a succinct reminder (Housman was a firm atheist) of the finitude of our lives — not original, of course, but as Doctor Johnson says, we need more often to be reminded than informed.

Nor is it true that Housman is always banal in the sense of saying what has been said many times before. Here is the tenth poem of his *Last Poems*:

> Could man be drunk for ever
>   With liquor, love or fights,
> Lief should I rouse at morning
>   And lief lie down at nights.
>
> But men at whiles are sober
>   And think in fits and starts,
> And if they think they fasten
>   Their hands upon their hearts.

The present moment often crowds out reflection; but when it does not, we are confronted by terror, remorse and regret.

If I had to interpret Connolly's assessment, I should put it like this: 'I may look like a pig, but at least I am superior to those who like Housman.'

My close friend and I share a little literary joke, or perhaps I should say a couple of catchphrases. Whenever we happen to talk about a choice between two more or less equal alternatives, we ask 'Fried or boiled?' And when we refer to a particularly fatuous or meaningless assertion, we say, 'His father is still very fond of meringues.'

These lines are from our favourite of Katherine Mansfield's stories, *The Daughters of the Late Colonel*, a beautiful and tragic study of the effect on the lives of two women of a domestic tyrant, their father the Colonel. They are Constance (Con) and Josephine (Jug), who are weak and indecisive because of circumstance but perhaps also because of character. They are incapable of deciding anything for themselves, having lived under the stentorian discipline of their father all their lives. When he dies, they are completely paralysed: they remind me of Paraguay after the death of Doctor José Gaspar Rodríguez de Francia, *El Supremo*, the Supreme One, its dictator of many years, when the population thought that his death might be a ruse to test its loyalty and to flush out those who rebelled in their hearts.

While the two daughters discuss the knotty problem of who shall have the late Colonel's gold watch, their servant Kate bursts through the door in her usual fashion, 'as if she had discovered some secret panel in the wall.' This always puts me in mind of my time as a patient in the Hospital for Tropical Diseases when regularly the tea-lady would burst into the small ward, crashing through its swing doors with her tea trolley as a kind of battering ram, and utter one single word: Tea'ncoffeemilk'nsugar?

Having burst into the room, Kate asks 'Fried or boiled?'

Fried or boiled? Josephine and Constance were quite bewildered for the moment. They could hardly take it in.

'Fried or boiled what, Kate?' asked Josephine, trying to concentrate.

Kate gave a loud sniff. 'Fish.'

So my friend and I, as an example of those arcane communications that are one of the pleasures of long intimacy, ask each other 'Fried or boiled?' A secret meaning obscure to outsiders is a seal of friendship.

As for the meringues, the quotation comes from the passage in the story when Cyril, the Colonel's grandson, visits the Colonel as he is dying. The Colonel is very deaf. Cyril can't think of anything to say, except that his father, the Colonel's son, is still very fond of meringues. The Colonel doesn't hear it the first time, and it has several times to be repeated until Cyril finally manages to make him hear it.

This always puts me in mind when, disgracefully, I was deputed as a medical student to inform a man's wife, waiting in a side-room, that there was no hope for her husband, that he was dying. Unfortunately, she was rather deaf and didn't hear what I said. She asked me to repeat myself, which I did. Still she did not hear, so I tried a third time to no better effect. Luckily, she had her daughter with her.

'What's he trying to say?' she asked her.

'He's trying to say that Dad's dying,' said the daughter in a voice that would have penetrated the Great Wall of China. And everyone was so relieved that the message had got through to the wife that its content was disregarded.

Katherine Mansfield uncovered significance, usually tragic, in the slight. In a few lines, the inevitable tragedy of human existence is revealed, often by a trivial circumstance or event.

In *Miss Brill*, a lonely single lady of a certain age goes out daily to walk along the promenade of a seaside town and amuses herself by watching the people go by. She persuades herself that it is a wonderful theatrical sight, so absorbing that it is a compensation, or more than a compensation, for the loneliness, the constriction, the uneventfulness of her own life. The illusion works until she overhears a young couple remarking on how absurd she looks. The scales fall from her eyes: but in effect we all need such scales. Who is it that lives completely without illusion?

Before taking her place on the promenade for the first time to watch the theatre of the world, Miss Brill donned her fox-fur:

> Miss Brill put up her hand and touched her fur. Dear little thing! It was nice to feel it again. She had taken it out of its box, shaken out the moth-powder, given it a good brush, and rubbed the life back into the dim little eyes.

Strange to relate, this took me back nearer seventy than sixty years, for my paternal grandmother, who like her husband had been a refugee from pogroms in Tsarist Russia, and who died more than sixty years ago, often wore a fox-fur, with the heads and tails (or brushes) of several foxes. As she always smelled of mothballs — camphor, now prohibited in Europe — I cannot say whether the fur smelled particularly of them, but I was always fascinated by the little glass bright eyes, amber and black, which seemed to me then masterpieces of the jeweller's art, since before you touched them, they might have been taken for real eyes.

The other thing that my grandmother wore that fascinated me was her hat pin, with which she fixed her flattish black hat with beads on to her coiffure. Out came the hat pin and off came the hat. The pin seemed to me of enormous size, at least relative to me, when almost everything looked large. At any rate, after her death, the pin in my imagination became a potentially formidable weapon, with which one could pierce a person's heart and thereby kill him or her.

My poor grandmother! She was dumpy and rather ill-favoured, and I suspect that her fox-fur, which would now strike young people as ridiculous if not the product of cruelty to foxes, represented for her the accession to bourgeois respectability, a kind of transitional object between persecution and safety, as a child hangs on to a soft toy as it separates a little from its mother. How I wished she were still alive, or had lived longer, so that she could have told me (in her bad English) what she had witnessed once I appreciated the importance of such testimony. What a safe and privileged life I have led without being in the slightest grateful for it!

I cannot completely convey or even explain the pleasure I had from reading *Miss Brill*, for such pleasure is non-transferable.

My copy of *The Garden Party and Other Stories* dates from 1924, being the sixth impression. It was first published in 1922, and on the flyleaf of my copy is written in brown ink, or ink that has gone brown, the name of a previous owner. He recorded the date, 2.10.1924, twenty-five years and nine days before I was born. His or her name was N. Chanter. Was this a real name, or a comment on the book, *Enchanter*?

Another thing I noticed about my copy: the head of the pages were gilded. I doubt that N. Chanter did this him- or herself. Therefore, a year after her death, 1923, Katherine Mansfield's work was regarded by her publisher, Constable and Company, as of more than usual worth.

I believe that the French author (who now lives in Belgium, possibly for tax reasons), Eric-Emmanuel Schmitt, is not highly regarded in French literary circles, for two main reasons: first, his work deals with philosophical questions but is popular and sells very well, and second (as a consequence) he has made a lot of money. It is not possible to starve in a garret any more, thanks to social security, but any self-respecting serious author ought to have a go at it.

His plays have been performed in fifty countries, though how many times I do not know. One of my books has been translated into Hungarian, but that does not make me well-known in Hungary. Be that as it may, I was in a bric-à-brac market of the market of St-Paul-le-Jeune when I came across the first volume of Schmitt's plays. *Fifty centimes*, said the owner of the stall.

Is it not strange how one sometimes dithers over spending 50 centimes when one regularly wastes incomparably more? Did I want the book, and if I bought it would I read it? If I bought it but did not read it, would that not be 50 centimes wasted? However, having started at the stall to read *Le Visiteur*

(The Visitor), a play about the last days of Sigmund Freud in Vienna, I decided to buy it, along with two other books at 1 euro each.

'Excuse me,' said the stall-owner's wife, 'I don't mean to intrude, but you have an accent.'

'English,' I replied.

'I lived in England for two years.'

'But you have an accent also.'

'I am Vietnamese.'

'When did you come to France?'

'1949.'

'I was born in that year.'

We were members of the 1949 community, then. All people who have anything in common these days are said to belong to the community of whatever they have in common: for lack of real community. I didn't stop to think of it at the time, but it was strange that she had an accent, for she must have been an infant when she came to France. She must have had a story to tell. Perhaps she spent her first years in a Vietnamese ghetto in France, these being the years of the Vietnamese war of independence.

Schmitt's play is interesting but not, to me, entirely satisfactory. Its first scene is entirely naturalistic, taking place in Freud's flat in the Berggasse. Freud's library has evidently been vandalised, and Freud and his daughter, Anna, discuss the question of leaving Vienna, now, after the Anschluss, ruled by the Nazis. Freud is reluctant because, aged and ill, he so loves Vienna, irrationally believing that no Viennese is a Nazi, and that Nazism is of entirely foreign imposition. Anna is more clear-sighted than her father: she knows that they must flee. Another of Freud's arguments against leaving is that to do so (his world- fame protecting him somewhat) would be to desert those left behind: and indeed, two of his sisters *were* murdered by the Nazis after his departure. The scene is perfectly plausible: reluctance to leave while it was still possible was quite common, composed as it was of fear of settling abroad late in life and the belief that the barbarism would soon be over and could hardly get worse, certainly not in countries as cultivated as Germany and Austria.

The play becomes unsatisfactory to me, perhaps because I tend to the literal-minded, when in the fourth scene (there are no acts, only scenes) an intruder arrives in the flat, Anna in the meantime having been taken away by the Gestapo. The intruder is known only as *L'Inconnu*, the Unknown person. At first, he is dressed as a dandy might be dressed at the opera before the war. He engages in long philosophical dialogues with Freud for the rest of the play.

But who is he? Is he real or an hallucination of Freud's? If he is real, the question arises as to his identity. Is he the madman who, we are told, has recently escaped from the local asylum, is he a burglar, or is he God or the Devil? If he is God, or the Devil, even as a mere hallucination on Freud's part, what does that tell us about Freud's famous atheism, according to which God is an imaginary, omnipotent father-figure who replaces the omnipotent father of the infant's imagination? It suggests that Freud's atheism was superficial, only skin-deep, and that he himself had not freed himself from the infantile desire for an omnipotent, benevolent authority figure to protect him from the dangers of the world.

Could it be, though, that the intruder is but a confidence

trickster? At the end of the play, Schmitt wants to leave all possibilities open, so that no definitive answer can be given as to the intruder's identity or ontological status. This seems to me to be a rather cheap form of intellectual sophistication, that involves evasion rather than genuine inquiry after truth.

But if Schmitt wanted to leave the question open, one detail betrays him. The intruder knows that Freud will soon live in Maresfield Gardens, Hampstead (in London), in a house which is now the Freud Museum. Freud, of course, does not know this himself. But how could anyone other than an omniscient being know the future with such exactitude? A charlatan or trickster would not venture on so specific a prophecy, or if he did, it would almost certainly turn out to be wrong. It is difficult, then, not to conclude that the intruder is actually God, the only omniscient being, the only being who could know that Freud would live in Maresfield Gardens.

It is possible that Schmitt intends us from this detail to conclude that God exists, and to tell us that in the dark (and at the time, Vienna was dark indeed) no man is an atheist, whatever his prior beliefs or philosophical arguments.

Another proof of the intruder's omniscience is that he knows that the title of the book Freud is then writing will be *Moses and Monotheism*, though Freud has not yet decided on such a title. Even psychoanalysts would not claim such detailed knowledge of a person's future.

One thing only remains in my memory of my visit to the Freud Museum in Maresfield Gardens (no doubt a fact of great psychological significance for searchers after meanings in the small change of life). I often find the book of comments at the end of an exhibition more interesting than the exhibition itself. A comment in the visitors' book of the Freud Museum immediately engraved itself on my memory: I'm glad he [Freud] wasn't *my* father.

Between the ages of 14 and 24 I kept a diary — a page a day, about 400 words. Then I stopped. I suppose I was too busy to continue, and by keeping it only intermittently I discovered what I had long suspected but not accepted: that it had been a chore and what I wrote was boring. Thirty years later, I looked into my diaries and was appalled by my former self. Censorious and humourless, my thoughts were entirely banal, no better or more interesting than the memoirs of the former Prime Minister, David Cameron, which it had been my misfortune to review (for money, of course). I threw my diaries away, but I should have burnt them. Sometimes my blood runs cold at the thought that someone might have rescued them from the dustbin into which I threw them and that they might one day resurface. My only consolation was that they were too boring to be used for blackmail. Carlyle once wrote that no one who was not a believer or a person with a professional interest could read the Koran, but my diaries were far worse even than that.

It was therefore with both admiration and envy that I read Joseph Kessel's notebook that he kept in November, 1914, when he was only sixteen. The entries were unpublished in his lifetime (1898-1979); they are very brief but far from trivial. On the contrary, they display an astonishing maturity of judgment as well as purity of style. He alights, as if by instinct, on the telling and the significant. His talent was obvious from a very early age: for it is rarely that a 16-year-old's reflections can be read more than a hundred years later with pleasure and even instruction.

Kessel must have been well taught. His father, a Russian Jewish doctor, emigrated to the Argentine, where Kessel was born, but they then returned to Russia, finally settling in France when Joseph was eight. Perhaps having French as a second, or even as a third, language was an advantage to him, since he had to learn it by conscious effort and could not just assume that he knew it perfectly because it was native to him. He attended a lycée in Nice, where the standards demanded of him would have been high.

Kessel had an astonishingly varied and adventurous life. Too young to enlist at once in the First World War, he served (as had Walt Whitman and Agatha Christie) as an assistant in a hospital for the wounded. Then he went to Paris, entering journalistic circles thanks to his mastery of Russian, a rare accomplishment at the time. He became an airman in the second half of the war, and after the war he travelled the world, attracted to remote places and danger. During the Second World War, he was in the Resistance. All his books — eighty in all — are from his personal experience, which was inexhaustible. His novels were in the realist mode, and he always wrote with the greatest clarity.

On November 6, 1914, he wrote:

> The head of the Krupp company has just received a doctorate from Bonn university. It is another manifestation of German 'Kultur' and proof of German intellectualism.

The 'short and brutal name' of Krupp 'evokes in a striking way the excellence that the German race accords to force that respects only force.'

But Kessel is aware, even at the age of 16, of the perils of chauvinism. On the day following, he wrote:

> At every kiosk, at every stationer's, collections of postcards spread their glaring colours whose overall effect is, so it seems, of a spiritual caricature. One sees Wilhelm adorned with horns or with a pig's head; one sees a German soldier rubbing his sides that have been hurt by the boot of a French soldier… And pictures of this type succeed one another in a truly astonishing diversity of stupidity.

If one believes that one proves one's patriotism by such pictures, he says, one is mistaken; on the contrary, they show how far the German spirit has invaded the French.

On 8 November, he reflects on the Tsar's prohibition of the sale of alcohol in the Russian empire. Drawing on his memory, the young Kessel writes:

> He who has seen the loving gesture of the drunk caressing his bottle [of vodka], and making the cork jump out of it with a single blow of the palm applied to its base will realise the the pleasure of which the Tsar has not hesitated to deprive the people.

But the young Kessel is not starry-eyed about the effects of alcohol:

He who has witnessed the procession of peasants, with serious faces, blond beards, broad-browed over dreamy eyes full of mysticism, entering the *traktir* [the inn or pub] and leaving unkempt and staggering will understand the ignoble transformation that alcohol produces in the soul of the peasant who is so peaceable, soft and idealistic.

According to Kessel, the prohibition was not without beneficial effect: peasants had more money to spend on essentials, and violence towards women declined. I saw a very similar effect on peasants in Guatemala when they were converted by very unattractive American evangelical missionaries: the difference being that the conversion was voluntary (though often the effect of bribery). In fact, though, the Tsar's prohibition was disastrous, as was later Gorbachev's. It reduced government revenue precisely at a time of increased expenditure, thereby contributing to the inflation that helped to undermine the government's authority. And, as readers of Venedikt Yerofeyev's *Moscow Stations* will know, Russians are highly ingenious when it comes to manufacturing alcohol in times of shortage.

One of the most remarkable items in Kessel's notebook of 1916, displaying an emotional maturity far greater than mine at a much more advanced age, is an account of what he witnessed while attending the wounded in Nice.

A young man, badly injured, was watched over by his wife most tenderly. She had come straight to his bedside despite the fact that he had abandoned her a few months before war broke out. A second woman arrives at his bedside, she for whom he had abandoned his wife. With admirable tolerance and, one might add, compassion, they agreed to work together, at least until he was fully healed — which, given the conditions of the time, might be never. In the face of death, quarrel is futile, and to maintain it is to invite permanent regret.

Kessel's maturity at the age of 16 was remarkable: his judgment, his empathy, his alertness to tragedy. It is difficult not to believe in his inborn talent, however propitious the times for its exercise.

While on the subject of Kessel, I will mention his short book, *In Syria*. He travelled there not long after the inauguration of the French mandate after the end of the First World War. He must have been one of the very few journalists actively to have dropped a bomb while on a journalistic voyage. He recounts the experience in a chapter titled *How I Bombed Suwayda*, then the capital of Druze territory. There is no chapter titled *Why I Bombed Suwayda*: one has to deduce the reasons from the rest of the text.

The Druze were very much opposed to the French mandate, but they seemed to have been equally opposed to everyone and everything else. It so happens that shortly before I read Kessel's little book, I read Eugène-Melchior de Vogüé's book about Syria and Lebanon written fifty years earlier, in which he described the massacre of 12,000 Christians by the Druze in Damascus. The whole Christian quarter of the city was destroyed: not that the Christians themselves had always been entirely pacific.

Kessel describes how General Gamelin had occupied

Suwayda before abandoning it (shades of the American withdrawal from Afghanistan). Kessel was flying in a plane whose pilot decided to make a detour so that he could drop a bomb on Suwayda, now that it was back in rebel hands. Kessel writes:

> And here, on the side of the mountain, the Druze capital. It is harsh and rough. At a clear distance from it is the Citadel which was devastated after General Gamelin left, having relieved its [besieged] French garrison.
>
> Now it was no longer a question of a tourist trip. My eyes sometimes fixed on the pilot, sometimes on the glass of the cockpit that allowed me to see the landscape clearly. I waited. For the bombing to succeed, it was a matter of seconds.
>
> I see the first house, the little gardens, from above. The pilot raises his arm, I pull on the handles. A column of smoke rises from the town, then another, and a third.
>
> Already, the aircraft changes direction.

Half an hour later, Kessel is in a bar, drinking in comradely fashion with the rest of the squadron.

It has often been remarked that modern warfare is possible because those who employ the weapons do not see the results close up. And in this little book, Kessel, who is a sensitive man, does not stop to consider the human consequences of his bomb on Suwayda. He wrote the book a century ago, and his detached account of the adventure offends modern sensibility. It seems to imply, by omission, that the sufferings of the Druze, killed or injured at random, do not count for anything.

Alternatively, they are collectively guilty by simple virtue of being Druze — the kind of supposition that we should now, rightly, reject. Alas, westerners are now often held to be guilty by simple virtue of being westerners. How does one defend oneself and one's country without resort to barbarism when such a view is held by enemies? It is a difficult question.

I visited Syria a little more than half a century after Kessel's book was published. It was in Hafez Assad's time, and Syria was then, as now, an appalling Baathist dictatorship. I suppose that I should therefore have hated it, but I found Damascus full of charm, at least in its daily life. I arrived late at my booked hotel, the *Venezia*, but my room was not ready, so heavy curtains were removed from the dining room windows and were spread on tables put together for me to rest on until my room was made ready.

Readiness was evidently a relative concept, for the bed had obviously been recently slept in, and there were the remains of a bread roll, complete with prickly crumbs, in it. However, I was accepting in those days; and I did not feel up to searching Damascus at midnight for somewhere better to sleep. In fact, I was still young enough to sleep soundly in such circumstances.

How times have changed (and not in all respects for the better)! Before boarding the Syrian Airways aircraft for India, whither I was bound, the passengers had to pick out their luggage displayed on the airport apron around the aircraft. This was on the theory, now completely outdated, that no one would explode the aircraft if he himself was on it. This seems almost quaintly rational!

After the publication of *In Syria*, Kessel wrote (in May, 1926) an article castigating French policy in the country. It was titled *Make the Necessary Effort or Abandon the Mandate*. It could be read as a criticism of western, especially American, meddling in the Middle East even now:

> So we are fighting in Syria, and we're going to fight some more…. In Syria there is an undeniable malaise, a crisis of confidence in the mandate power… How have we arrived here? How can we get out of this situation?

Kessel's explanation is that France is prepared to commit neither the money nor the men to make a success of the mandate, and that furthermore the constant change of staff at the top means that as soon as they get some grasp of the complexity of the country that they have been called upon to rule, they are moved elsewhere. There are some men, lower in the hierarchy, fluent Arabic-speakers, who know their little area intimately and make themselves respected by the local notables, but there is no overall direction to their work. Kessel never asks the question of why the French should be in Syria at all. The nearest he comes to suggesting a reason is because the British (*les anglais*) are in Iraq.

> The necessary effort of money and men. Why have the Druze rebels, who are not even ten thousand, been able to disturb the peace of a vast country? Because they have the impression that France either does not want or cannot be bothered to go to the end.

Surely the people in the Middle East who are so inclined know that the Americans have neither the means nor the will to occupy their lands long-term? And they have been proved right. Kessel says it is better to abandon the game than play it badly. At the beginning of his book, he says:

> This cradle of civilisations, this predestined crossroads, whose wealth and beauty has retained, without mixing, so many peoples, this land whose beliefs and heresies have grown with such force, disturbs and confuses.

Plus ça change.

The fourth book I bought in Nîmes, the one that led the bookseller to conclude that I was a bibliophile, was an edition of *Athinea* by Charles Maurras. It was first published in 1896, but this edition was published in 1926. It was expensively rebound: the French had long published books only in paperback, leaving it to the purchasers to rebind them (or not), according to their taste, often bad, or to their means.

I was attracted to this copy because it had a dedication by the author. Unfortunately, his handwriting was so bad that it was not possible, for me at least, to make out in its entirety what he had written. The best I could do was: To Doctor Roger Lefevre, in memory of a splendid banquet of 19 February 1928, the cordial tribute of the author. It was all such a scrawl that it gives the impression that signing books was a bore for him, and he even made a spelling mistake — *homage* in place of *hommage*.

Maurras was a founder of *Action française*, the nationalist and proto-fascist movement. He was a monarchist and very pro-Catholic, though for most of his adult life he had very little real religious belief. Like many conservatives, he thought that religion was essential for the maintenance of an ordered and civilised society (had he been born in an Islamic country he would have been an Islamist). Insofar as such people observe religious ritual, they do so more for the sake of order and tradition than because they believe in the truth of the doctrine.

Athinea is a collection of articles about the relation of French culture to the Roman Mediterranean civilisation. For Maurras, all that comes from the north, especially from Germany, is barbarism. Having been struck by deafness early in life, he makes no mention of the German contribution to music, which is possibly greater than that of all other nations combined — if one includes Austria. Of Britain and America, he is hardly complimentary.

There are in the book dithyrambs to the landscape of the Mediterranean coast and hinterland which are entirely sincere. Part of the book is an account of a journey to modern Athens. Even here, he cannot quite refrain from indulging in his fervent antisemitism. Here is the passage in which he describes the modern Athenian museum of antiquities:

> Our museum of the Louvre, above all in the section of ancient sculpture, offers at first sight a horrible image of clutter. Not that order is missing there: only that the key to this order is not put into the hand of everyone. In every Athenian museum, to the contrary, the child or the ignorant person has only to look about him, not only to be pleased, but to be able to order and reason about his

impressions.

Hypothetical order, no doubt, entirely inductive attributions, but necessary. A tour takes the place of much reading. We see there the living history of the sculptural art of the ancient Greeks.

The honour for this beautiful order belongs to M. Carvadias, the general curator of antiquities in the Kingdom of Greece. M. Salomon Reinsch has praised him with great warmth. One whispers in Paris that the compliment is only self-praise. M. Reinsch was the adviser and even the assistant and inspirer of M. Carvadias. Think what you like of this rumour, personally I pay it little attention. Why should an Athenian of good descent not have dated the national Antiquities without having had a Jew as a deputy or master?

There is, of course, an entire theory behind this question. In fact, Salomon Reinsch was a very distinguished archaeologist and scholar (far more distinguished in the field than was Maurras, who, however, was very far from an ignorant man). He was, moreover, the first translator of Schopenhauer into French. The theory behind Maurras's question is that a past culture can only *really* be understood by someone who is a biological descendent of the people of that culture, no matter how remote from the present-day that culture, while a non-descendent, no matter how learned, cannot understand it. Understanding, then, comes through the blood rather than the mind: a theory which we might decry both as absurd and nasty but which has been revivified by identity politicians, with their objections to so-called 'cultural appropriation'.

Salomon Reinsch was the brother of Joseph, the chronicler in six large volumes of the Dreyfus Affair, and strong opponent of Maurras — who thought that the honour of the army was more important than the individual fate of Dreyfus: in other words, that to condemn an innocent man to solitary confinement on Devil's Island for the rest of his life was somehow to defend the honour of the institution that sent him there, a concept of honour not more sophisticated than that of those who killed girls of Pakistani origin because they would not marry whoever their father said they should marry. When Maurras wrote his *Athinea*, the Affair had not yet reached its apogee.

Some of the most interesting pages of the book are about the first modern Olympic Games, held in Athens in 1896. The population of Athens at the time was 120,000, and 80,000 people (according to Maurras) attended the games. What most surprised me about Maurras's account — that of a highly intelligent and cultivated, if prejudiced, man — was that it demonstrated that from the very first the games were a means of expressing fervent nationalism. The winner of an event was taken as proof of national power and prowess, if not of outright superiority. I had rather supposed that the games had been friendly rather than intensely rivalrous, but I was mistaken.

Maurras tells a very amusing story about the marathon run at the games. The Greek crowd in the stadium where the marathon was to end was delirious with joy when it was a Greek who won. The next seven behind the winner were also Greek, but the winner was of much lower social class than they.

Mademoiselle Y…. [a young lady of high class], as patriotic as she was beautiful, had heard of the patriotism of antiquity. The day before the race, she publicly swore that she would bestow her hand on the winner if he were Greek.

Mademoiselle Y…. could permit herself, without too great a risk, to so serious an undertaking: it was known that the great majority of champions, all young men of good appearance, belonged to excellent families, being students or officers… and here was a herdsman who had won.

Everyone in Athens — everyone in *le tout Paris* sense, that is — was laughing, and the young lady herself was torn between the desire to release herself from her public promise and the duty to keep it.

I have mentioned that Henry James once said that Edmund Gosse (1849-1928), the literary critic, essayist, biographer and memoirist, had a genius for inaccuracy. Nevertheless, he was an excellent stylist, and his literary criticism is still a pleasure to read. Even if he was inaccurate, he was erudite and very well read — in several languages. Whether erudition is worth the effort to acquire it, when it will all be lost, and much of the knowledge acquired will come to seem mere pedantry, or unimportant, in a few years' time, I do not know. I doubt whether any literary critic alive today knows as much as Gosse did, if for no other reason than that Gosse always had servants to take care of the time-consuming and boring quotidian tasks that now take up so much of our time and energy.

I write this on the centenary of the publication of one of his volumes of collected essays, titled *More Books on the Table*. Like my patient who deduced from the fact that there had been a second world war that there must have been a first, I deduced that there must also have been a book of Gosse's titled *Books on the Table*. When I opened my copy of *More Books*, I was soon laughing.

It was a short essay (all the essays in the book are short) titled *Snap-Shots at Swinburne*, that made me laugh. The essay was a review of Mrs Watts-Dunton's memoir of the famous poet, a memoir titled *The Home Life of Swinburne*. The poet died, by the way, on the day my father was born.

At the age of 42, Swinburne, exhausted by a life of drinking, flagellation and dissolution, went to live with Mr and Mrs Watts-Dunton in Putney; and while his dissolute life inspired, or was coterminous with, much poetry, his respectable and healthy life with the Watts-Duntons thereafter inspired much less poetry, and that little of inferior quality.

Mrs Watts-Dunton published her memoir of Swinburne thirteen years after his death. Gosse had written a life of Swinburne, so even with his supposed genius for inaccuracy, must have been well-qualified as a reviewer. Of Mrs Watts-Dunton's memoir he writes:

> There is no malice and plenty of good humour… in the pages of this so-called *Home Life*. But surely, no great man was ever more completely shorn of the mystery which his admirers loved to weave about him…. We see the poet "partaking of the biggest fattest gooseberries I have ever

seen." We may miss the laurel and the glory, but Swinburne stands revealed before us, "waving his hand towards the jam and the hock," and "airily saying, 'Shall we have luncheon now?'"

Of course, even poets must eat lunch, and Gosse continues:

I am far from despising these details, nor does it shock me to be told that the great poet "braces his trousers too high." Or that his locks, once so redundant and so umbrageous, were, in later years, "often cut by the barber."

Here I may intrude an inconsequential memory of my own. I recall the time when all my uncles, particularly my Uncle Joe, a man of the sweetest disposition, 'braced their trousers too high', so that they came halfway up their chests. My Uncle Nat, whose precise relationship to me I never understood, also braced his trousers too high, but I remember him for something else, namely that he was suspected briefly of murder because of the motiveless malice of his neighbours. A maid of his was 'walking out', as they put it in those days, with a young man who visited her one evening when my uncle and his wife were out. The young man strangled her and then walked out of the flat in my uncle's hat. Some of the neighbours saw this but testified that they had seen my uncle, not merely the hat, so that suspicion fell on him, though it was soon to be lifted. But it left a bitter aftertaste that people, previously friendly and polite, were so willing, and so quickly, to believe the worst of him.

The trousers 'braced too high' were not exactly a fashion, at least in its most whimsical sense — my uncles were not followers of fashion, exactly — but more an accepted way to dress. But I remember that these trousers fascinated me.

Back to Gosse. He writes:

> Let it not be imagined for a moment that I am reproving these revelations. On the contrary, I delight in them, as I delight in the snap-shots of the newspapers.

On the other hand:

> I cannot expel from my mind the contrast between the dignity of the poet's calling and the charming triviality of these anecdotes.

Perhaps the charming triviality is the forerunner of what might be called the feet-of-clay school of biography, in which the previously unsuspected foibles or vices of a great man are displayed for the delectation of the common reader, who is then enabled to indulge in a false syllogism:

> The great man had such-and-such a vice.
> I have such-and-such a vice.
> Therefore, I am a great man.

Gosse raises the interesting question as to the relation of small truths in biography to the overall truth of a person's life. The book under review, moreover, relates small matters and conversations at a considerable distance in time. 'The very minuteness of the record here… creates in the mind of the reader a faint atmosphere of doubt,' writes Gosse. Yet 'what matters is the picture of the man, and this seems on the whole to be accurate.' Errors as to the detail, accuracy as to the whole: this is a curious idea, yet we all know what it means and agree with it in practice.

There is in the book an essay on A.E. Housman (who then had still thirteen years to live). It is very judicious.

> There is something to be said for a formula that explains such wide expanses as the work of Browning and Victor Hugo, but intensity may be gained at the expense of breadth… He [Housman] is the port of *desideratum*, of the unconquerable longing for what is gone for ever, for youth which has vanished, for friends that are dead, for beauty that was a mirage.

Gosse here captures the essence of Housman that Connolly missed. I would add that poetry for me is more for depth of feeling than breadth of feeling, which so rapidly becomes cant.

Reviewing Lytton Strachey's biography of Queen Victoria, Gosse says of the death of that Queen:

> More than twenty years divide us from an event which was calculated to disturb the balance of judgment in a very unusual degree… In the Ciceronian phrase, she [the Queen] had completed a voyage that was long and rough, and now she had sighted land and had entered port. But although this is a common lot of man, the world had ceased to be convinced that Victoria would undergo

it. Logically, no one was foolish enough to conceive that she would live for ever, but sentimentally she had come to seem sempiternal, a portion of the order of things...

How strange that, a hundred years later, I could have written the same about the death of Elizabeth II, in whose reign I had lived seventy of my seventy-three years! She was 'a portion of the order of things', or at any rate of *my* order of things. I had hoped that she would outlast me, a foolish wish, no doubt, but a tribute to a head of state who had never oppressed me or caused me a moment's anxiety or disquiet: surely not something very common in human history.

I have come nearly to the end of my notebook, and so I will conclude, as in my last book of this genre, with something about Dylan Thomas, from whose poem I have taken my title. It seems only fair.

Dylan Thomas is not normally thought of as a political writer, much less as a prophet: he is, if anything, more religious in nature, certainly contemplative, almost politically quietist. His political views, such as they were, were vaguely left-wing, but so were those of practically all intellectuals in his day, perhaps understandably so. He was born, after all, in the year of the outbreak of the First World War, and by the time he looked around him, it was the Great Depression, which struck South Wales, where he lived, with the greatest force. It was obvious that all was not going well in the world, and it was only natural that people should desire a fundamental change in the way in which it was organised (they assumed, of course, that it *was* organised). But Dylan Thomas was only marginally interested in politics, and his ideas on that subject were neither deeply thought nor deeply felt.

But he did write one poem, published in 1935, that seems prophetic: *The Hand that Signed the Paper*. Its first line is, 'The hand that signed the paper felled a city…' Here is what, many years later, Hannah Arendt was to call 'the banality of evil.' Actually, she was mistaken in the circumstances of her usage of it: she fell for Eichmann's self-presentation as a faceless bureaucrat, pushing papers about according to orders without any emotional connection to what was done as a consequence. Eichmann was, in fact, a far more ideologically-committed man than this suggests. She was duped by him in the same way that Margaret Mead was duped by the Samoans when they pretended to be complete sexual libertines.

Nevertheless, Thomas's first line does draw attention to the power of a single person to do great evil at the stroke of a pen, without having to witness it himself. He can sit in his office and order murder and destruction; he may be squeamish personally and yet cover the world in blood. This is one reason why absolute power is so dangerous. A dictator can 'Double the globe of dead and halve a country', and yet live like the most prudish or punctilious petit bourgeois.

'The mighty hand leads to the sloping shoulder,' says the poem, and this is a very accurate and succinct observation. I am not philologist enough to know whether the expression *sloping shoulder* was in wide use when Thomas wrote his poem, but certainly I heard it used often (and saw the phenomenon, too) in my career.

A sloping shoulder is a refusal to take moral responsibility for one's actions within a hierarchy where there are persons superior to oneself in that hierarchy. One is only 'obeying orders' and therefore not truly responsible for one's actions. The person who *is* responsible often cannot be found. (The slope can also go in a downward direction.) The person at the top of the hierarchy will claim not to know what is being done in his name; but everyone below him is only obeying orders. Thus responsibility itself disappears.

The matter is not straightforward. Almost everyone would agree that there have to be hierarchies in the world, that no organisation above a certain size can abjure them completely: and hierarchies cannot exist without obedience. Ultimately, someone, somewhere, must have the say. But:

> Great is the hand that holds dominion over
> Man by a scribbled name…

A perfect excuse for the worst behaviour is then always to hand. Every act by every person except the possessor of that great hand can claim to have been done under duress of one kind or another, even if the evil done is a great pleasure, as it often is.

The ultimate great hands when the poem was published were Hitler and Stalin. Their power was eventually so great that they did not even have to sign the paper for their wishes to be obeyed. Did Thomas have them in mind when he wrote the poem? He wrote it in 1933, when the full extent of Nazi malevolence could hardly have been known, only surmised.

I have come to the end of my notebook. By stopping, I am obeying an order: admittedly an order made up and imposed by me on myself.

www.ingramcontent.com/pod-product-compliance
Lightning Source LLC
LaVergne TN
LVHW041212080426
835508LV00011B/925